Spanish Grammar: A Quick Reference

David Wren

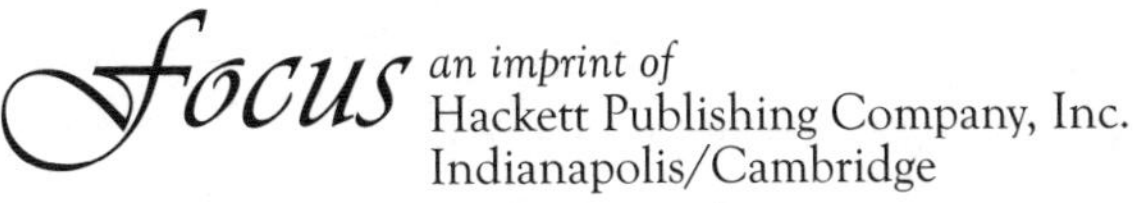
an imprint of
Hackett Publishing Company, Inc.
Indianapolis/Cambridge

A Focus book

Focus an imprint of
Hackett Publishing Company

Printed in the United States of America

21 20 19 18 1 2 3 4 5 6 7

For further information, please address
Hackett Publishing Company, Inc.
P.O. Box 44937
Indianapolis, Indiana 46244-0937

www.hackettpublishing.com

Cover design by Rick Todhunter
Composition by Integrated Composition Systems

Cataloging-in-Publication data can be accessed via the Library of Congress Online Catalog.

ISBN-13: 978-1-58510-899-2

The paper used in this publication meets the minimum requirements of American National Standard for Information Sciences—Permanence of Paper for Printed Library Materials, ANSI Z39.48–1984.

∞

Contents

PART 1: GENERAL GRAMMAR

PART 2: VERB FORMS

Overview of the Spanish Verb System

Verb Forms, Conjugated in all Tenses

Simple Tenses

Compound Tenses

Irregular Verbs: Lists and Patterns

PART 3: USES OF THE VERB TENSES

For additional resources—including more detailed presentations, interactive grammar and vocabulary exercises, pronunciation drills, and more—visit www.hackettpublishing.com/spanish-grammar-resources.

PART 1: GENERAL GRAMMAR

1-1. The Spanish Alphabet

The alphabet has **30 symbols**; three are pairs of letters representing one sound.

Letter	Spanish Name	Examples/Notes
a	**a**	**as in f*a*ther**
b	**be (larga/grande)**	**beber**[1]
c	**ce**	**s/th/k**[2]
ch	**che**	**China**
d	**de**	**dedo**
e	**e**	**as in b*e*t**
f	**efe**	**fotografía**
g	**ge [heh]**	**gigante**[3]
h	**hache**	**Héctor**[4]
i	**i (latina)**	**civil**
j	**jota [ho-tah]**	**Juan**[3]
k	**ka**	**kilo**[5]
l	**ele**	**Lalo**
ll	**elle [eh-yeh]**	**ella**
m	**eme**	**momento**
n	**ene**	**nota**
ñ	**eñe [eh-nyeh]**	**año**
o	**o**	**como**
p	**pe**	**pipa**
q	**cu**	**que; quinto**[6]
r	**ere**	***tt* in bu*tt*er**
rr	**erre**	**trilled *r***[7]
s	**ese**	**sesos**
t	**te**	**tutear**
u	**u**	**Uruguay**
v	**uve, ve (chica)**	**vivo**[1]
w	**doble ve, ve doble**	**Washington**[5]
x	**equis**	**[ks]; [s]**[8]
y	**i griega**	**Yucatán**
z	**zeta**	**s/th**[9]

1: *b, v* are generally pronounced the same
2: *c* before *e* or *i* = *s* in Lat. Am., *th* (*bath*) in Spain; before *a, o, u* = *k* everywhere
3: *g* before *e, i* = *jota* sound; hard *g* before *a, o, u*; *j* always = *jota*. Hard *g* before *e, i* spelled with silent *u*: *llegue, guía*
4: *h* always silent
5: *k, w* used only in foreign words
6: *que* = *keh*; *qui* = *kē*
7: Initial *r* (*Ricardo*) also trilled
8: = *ks* between vowels (*exacto*), *s* or *ks* before a consonant (*extender*)
9: = *s* in Lat. Am., *th* (*bath*) in Spain

1-2. Capitalization

Caps used **much less than** in English. Like English, used in first word of sentence, and in personal and place names:

> **La** chica y **Ana** son de **Puerto Rico.**

Caps **not** used in words referring to:

- months, days of week:
  enero, febrero... lunes, martes...

- language; national or regional origin:
  Los **mexicanos** hablan **español**.

  Soy de Asturias; soy **asturiano/a**.

- political, religious, academic association:
  Cree en el **cristianismo**; es **cristiano/a**.

  una obra **shakespeariana**

  los **demócratas** y los **republicanos**

- personal or official titles:
  el **presidente** Lincoln

  el **señor** / la **señora** Rodríguez

- titles, other than in the first word:
  La guerra de las galaxias (*Star Wars*)

1-3. Punctuation

Similar to English; some differences:

- **¿** and **¡** precede questions and exclamations:
  ¡Hola! ¿Qué tal?

  ¡Qué bien hablas! ¿Dónde estudiaste?

- **Colon** (:) used after greeting of letter, formal or informal:
  Muy señor mío: Querida Alicia:

- ***Raya*** (—) used for dialogue:
  —No, dijo Alberto—. No voy.

- ***Comillas*** (« ») used to highlight word(s) or for a quote within a quote:
  No menciones la palabra «*béisbol*».

  Siempre le digo: «*cállate*».

1-4. Syllabification, Stress and Accents

a. Syllable Division

Vowels

- Single vowels belong to one syllable:
  ca-pi-tal a-trac-ti-vo
- Adjacent "strong" vowels (*a, e, o*) form part of separate syllables:
  le-o em-ple-ar
- "Strong" + "weak" (*i, u*) combination form diphthong, belong to one syllable:
  vein-te duer-mo

  pa-tio cuo-ta

Consonants

- Single consonants (including *rr, ch, ll*) go with following syllable:
  ca-mi-sa vo-lu-men

  ca-ña pe-rri-to

  mu-cha-cha ca-lle
- Pairs in which the second consonant is *l* or *r* go with following syllable:
  ha-blo pa-dre

  fla-gran-te a-pli-car
- Other consonants pairs split up:
  mar-tes an-tes

  cam-bia ap-to
- Three-consonant combinations of which the last is *l* or *r* divide after first letter:
  hom-bre an-cla
- Other three-consonant combinations divide after second letter:
  trans-fe-rir ins-ti-tu-to
- Four-consonant combinations are divided in the middle:
  ins-tru-ir trans-cri-bir

b. Stress Rules

STRESS falls on a vowel of most words. Some words—such as *de, el, en, que*—are unstressed.

Rules for Normal Stress

Words ending in:

1. **A vowel, *n* or *s***—stressed on **second-to-last syllable**:

car-ta	a-trac-ti-vo
ha-bla-mos	can-tan

2. **Other letter**—stressed on **last syllable**:

tra-er	li-be-ral
na-riz	co-ñac

c. Use of Written Accents

An accent is placed on the stressed vowel of a word in the following cases:

1. Word violates a stress rule (see above):

Violate **Rule 1**

in-glés	ca-pi-tán
his-tó-ri-ca	ar-tí-cu-lo
dá-me-la	sen-tán-do-se

Note: *-mente* adverbs have normal stress, but keep adjectives' original accent, if any:

rápido → rápidamente

espontáneo → espontáneamente

Violate **Rule 2**

ár-bol	Gon-zá-lez
ca-rác-ter	ré-cord

2. Stressed "weak" vowel (*i, u*) is adjacent to a "strong" vowel (*a, e, o*):

o-í-mos	Ma-rí-a
gra-dú-a	Ra-úl

3. Word is interrogative or exclamatory:
¿**Cuándo** vas? ¿**Dónde** vives?

¡**Qué** inteligente es Ricardo!

¡**Cuánto** come tu hermanito!

Implied interrogatives also have accent:
No sé **qué** hora es.

I don't know ***what*** *time it is.*

Pregúntale **cuándo** quiere salir.

Ask him ***when*** *he wants to leave.*

Corresponding non-interrogatives have no accent:
La casa **donde** vivo está allí.

Cuando veo a José, lo saludo.

La chica con **quien** hablé se llama Irma.

4. A stressed word has a non-stressed counterpart that is spelled the same:

de (prep.) **dé** (verb)

el (article) **él** (pron.)

mi (adj.) **mí** (pron.)

se (pron.) **sé** (verb)

si (*if*) **sí** (*yes*)

solo (adj.) **sólo** (adv.)

te (pron.) **té** (*tea*)

tu (adj.) **tú** (pron.)

ACCENT "LOSS" OR "GAIN"

- **Some words with rule-breaking singular forms "lose" the accent in plural or feminine forms that comply with rule:**
  inglés → inglesa/ingleses/inglesas
  nación → naciones autobús → autobuses
- **Others whose singular forms comply with rules "gain" an accent in a rule-breaking plural form:**
  joven → jóvenes origen → orígenes
  See stress rules under 1-4b

1-5. Numbers

a. Cardinal Numbers

(0-20)

0 cero	
1 un(o)*	11 once
2 dos	12 doce
3 tres	13 trece
4 cuatro	14 catorce
5 cinco	15 quince
6 seis	16 dieciséis
7 siete	17 diecisiete
8 ocho	18 dieciocho
9 nueve	19 diecinueve
10 diez	20 veinte

(21-40)

21 veintiun(o)*	31 treinta y un(o)*
22 veintidós	32 treinta y dos
23 veintitrés	33 treinta y tres
24 veinticuatro	34 treinta y cuatro
25 veinticinco	35 treinta y cinco
26 veintiséis	36 treinta y seis
27 veintisiete	37 treinta y siete
28 veintiocho	38 treinta y ocho
29 veintinueve	39 treinta y nueve
30 treinta	40 cuarenta

****UNO/-UNO***
Appear only as masculine pronoun;
***un, -ún,* used otherwise:**
¿*Un* dólar? ¿Solamente *uno*?
¿Tienes *veintiún* años o *treinta y uno*?

(50-100)

50	cincuenta	80	ochenta
60	sesenta	90	noventa
70	setenta	100	cien

(101-199)

101 ciento uno

102 ciento dos

120 ciento veinte

199 ciento noventa y nueve

(200–900: note **irregular forms**)

200	doscientos(as)*	600	seiscientos(as)
300	trescientos(as)	700	**setecientos(as)**
400	cuatrocientos(as)	800	ochocientos(as)
500	**quinientos(as)**	900	**novecientos(as)**

AGREEMENT WITH *100*s

Multiples of *100* show gender agreement with noun, whether noun appears or not:

***Doscientos* hombres trabajan aquí.**

¿Mujeres? Hay *trescientas* (mujeres).

Exception:

No agreement if number follows noun:

Leí doscientas diez páginas. (210 pages)

But: Leí la página doscientos diez. (p. 210)

(1000 +)

1.000[1]	mil[2]
2.000...9.000	dos, tres...nueve mil
10.000	diez mil
100.000	cien mil
1.000.000	un[2] millón (de)[3]

1: In most Spanish-speaking countries, *period* and *comma* are the reverse of English:
5.012 = five thousand twelve
5,012 = five and twelve thousandths

2: *un* used with *millón, billón*, but not with *mil*

3: *de* used between *millón, billón* and noun:
dos millones / billones *de* dólares

2.000.000	dos millones (de)
10.000.000	diez millones (de)
100.000.000	cien millones (de)
1.000.000.000	mil millones (de)[4]
1.000.000.000.000	un[2] billón (de)[4]

4: Sp. *billón* = Eng. *trillion*

b. Ordinal Numbers

1st	primero	6th	sexto
2nd	segundo	7th	séptimo
3rd	tercero	8th	octavo
4th	cuarto	9th	noveno
5th	quinto	10th	décimo

MORE ABOUT ORDINAL NUMBERS

Not used with dates except for *first*:

Sept. 1: el *primero* de septiembre
Sept. 2: el *dos* de septiembre

Agree in gender as adjectives or pronouns:

el quinto (capítulo) / la quinta (página)

***Primer, tercer* used before masc. sing. nouns:**

el primer / tercer libro

Above 10th, cardinals are generally used:

el piso *once*	**the *eleventh* floor**
el cliente *cien*	**the *100th* customer**

Abbreviated with numerals plus *o, a*:

5º piso   4ª casa

1-6. Articles

a. Definite Articles: Forms

	Masc.	Fem.
Sing.	**el**	**la**
Plur.	**los**	**las**

b. Definite Articles: Uses

Where English uses a definite article, Spanish usually does also:

Yo comí **el** helado y él comió **la** fruta.

I ate the ice cream and he ate the fruit.

Exception: with names of monarchs:

Carlos Quinto   *Charles* ***the*** *Fifth*

But: Spanish often uses article where English does not:

- With days of week (= *on*):
  el lunes, etc.   *on Monday*, etc...

  los lunes, etc.   *on Mondays*, etc...

- Generic, categorical references:
  Los limones y **las** naranjas son frutas.

  Lemons and oranges are fruits.

  La historia es fascinante.

  History is fascinating.

- With the hour when giving the time:
  a **la una** / a **las dos**...   (*at one, at two...*)

- Before each noun in a series, esp. when gender changes:
  la taza y **el** platillo   (*the cup and saucer*)

- With some place names:
  la Argentina   **la** Habana   **el** Perú

- With some nouns referring to institutions:
  Voy a **la** escuela / a **la** iglesia.

  I go to school/church.

  Está en **la** cárcel.

  He's in prison.

- With common personal titles:
  La señora / **el** señor Ruiz está presente.

  Déselo **al** profesor / a **la** profesora Díaz.

Exceptions: direct address; *don, doña*:
Buenos días, señor / señora Alarcón.

Conozco a don Gustavo y a doña Alicia.

- With an infinitive used as generic:
  El correr es bueno para la salud.

  Running is good for one's health.

- With name of language:
  El español y **el** inglés son diferentes.

  Spanish and English are different.

Exceptions: After *en*, *de*, and *hablar*:
Hablo español pero soy maestro de inglés.   Dímelo en inglés.

- Instead of indefinite article with weights, measures (= *per*):
  un dólar **el** litro / **la** libra (*a liter/pound*)

- Instead of possessive with body parts, clothing:
  Me rompí **la** pierna y **el** brazo.

  I broke my leg and my arm.

  Ponte **la** camisa y **los** zapatos.

  Put on your shirt and your shoes.

Obligatory[1] Contractions with *el*[2, 3]

a + el→al ***de + el→del***

1. English offers choice: *do not* or *don't*
2. *la, los, las* and pronoun *él* do not contract:
   a la ciudad; la historia *de las* ciudades
   El libro es *de él*.   *A él* no le gusta el libro.
3. Exception: *El* doesn't contract if part of name or title:
   Fuimos a El Salvador.
   Tengo una copia de «*El mundo es ansí*».

c. Neuter Article *lo*

Used with masculine singular adjectives[1] and adverbs[2] referring to abstract qualities; with variable adjectives[3] referring to specific noun:

Lo extraño[1] de eso es que...

The strange thing about that is that...

lo trágico[1] y **lo cómico**[1] en sus novelas...

tragic and comical elements in his novels...

¡Mira **lo bien**[2] que juegan esos niños!

Look how well those kids play!

Vimos **lo listas**[3] que son las chicas.

We saw how smart the girls are.

d. Indefinite Articles: Forms

	Masc.	Fem.
Sing.	**un***	**una**
Plur.	**unos**	**unas**

* *Uno* used as pronoun, not as article:
El tiene dos coches; yo tengo *uno*.

e. Indefinite Articles: Uses

Some differences with English usage:

► Usually repeated in a series:
una taza y **un** platillo *a cup and saucer*

Often omitted where English uses it:

► Before unmodified noun following *ser*:

Es médico. *He's a doctor.*

Soy mujer. *I'm a woman.*

But: Es un médico competente.

► Often after *tener, llevar, haber, sin*:

No tengo pluma. *I have no pen.*

¿Hay coche? *Is there a car?*

Llevo corbata. *I wear a tie.*

sin billete *without a ticket*

But: Article used with modified nouns, or if *number* one is stressed:

Hay **un** coche azul.

Tengo *una* hermana. (*one*, not *two*)

sin *un* centavo

► After *como, medio, ¡qué!*:

Vine como alumno *...as a student*

media hora *...half an hour*

¡Qué buen tipo! *What a good guy!*

► Before or after *cien, mil, otro, tal*:

tal persona *such a person*

Dame otro. *Give me another one.*

Plural forms *unos, unas*

= *some; a few; approximately*:

Tengo unas cartas y unos sobres.

Vienen unas trescientas personas.

1-7. Gender of Nouns

a. Masculine Nouns

- Most nouns ending in *-o*:
  el libro   *el* chico   *el* río

  Exceptions:

  la mano   *a* foto(grafía)   *la* moto(cicleta)

- All months, days of week:
  el enero, febrero, etc.

  el lunes, martes, etc.

- Numbers:
  el dos de mayo

  Escribo *un 6* en la pizarra.

- Nouns ending in *-aje, -or*:
  el equipaje   *el* color

  Exceptions:

  la flor   *la* labor

b. Feminine Nouns

Most nouns ending in *-a*:
la pluma   *la* chica   *la* casa

Exceptions (masc.):

clima	papá	problema
día	planeta	sistema
drama	poema	sofá
¡**Buenos** días!	Siéntese en **el** sofá.	

Letters of the alphabet:
la «b» larga   *una «f»* minúscula

Nouns ending in:
-dad, -tad, -tud, -ie, -sis, -umbre, -ión

la verdad	*la* tesis
la libertad	*la* costumbre
la actitud	*la* tensión
la serie	*la* nación

Exceptions (masc.):
camión, avión, análisis, énfasis

Use of *el, un* with Feminine Nouns

Immediately preceding nouns starting with stressed *a-*, *ha-*:
el águila **un** hacha

But: **la** magnífica águila
las águilas **unas** hachas

c. Nouns of Variable Gender

Many *-a* nouns referring to persons are either *m.* or *f.*:
el/la: atleta, poeta, dentista, socialista

un(a) buen(a) artista

*-nte** nouns:
el/la: amante, adolescente, agente, etc.

*But note: el presidente, la presidenta, el asistente, la asistenta

Some *-o* nouns of occupation:
el/la: piloto músico soldado

Notes:
Use varies between *la médica; la abogada for females;* and *el/la médico, el/la abogado*
Other occupations have *-o/-a* variation:
el/la biólogo/a, el/la psicólogo/a

Other words:
el/la: líder, joven, intérprete

arte: masc. in singular, fem. in plural:

el arte francés; las bellas artes

1-8. Noun and Adjective Plurals

▸ Add *-s*:

Words that end in unstressed vowel; stressed *a* or *e*:

guapa(s)	serie(s)	tribu(s)	bici(s)
sofá(s)	papá(s)	café(s)	pie(s)

▸ Add *-es*:

Words ending in *y*; a consonant except *s*; stressed vowel + *s*; stressed *i* or *u*:

color(es)	rey(es)	español(es)
virtud(es)	inglés→ingleses	
vez→veces[1]	esquí(es)	tabú(es)[2]

1: *z*→*c* in *-z* nouns: *feliz*→*felices*
2: But: *menú*→*menús*

Loan Words

Some add *-s*, others *-es*

hit(s)	coñac(s)	boicot(s)
álbum(es)	bar(es)	dólar(es)

Nouns Identical in Singular and Plural

▸ Nouns ending in unstressed vowel + *s*:

el/los análisis	*la/las* hipótesis
el/los:	lunes, martes, miércoles, jueves, viernes
el/los:	lavaplatos, abrelatas, paraguas

▸ Surnames:

los González   los Smith   los Jones

1-9. Adjective Forms

a. 4-form Adjectives

(Agree with noun in *number* and *gender*)

Masculine singular *-o, -és*[1], *-án, -ón, -or*:

Masc. Sing.	Fem. Sing	Masc. Pl.	Fem. Pl.
guap**o**[2]	**-a**	**-os**	**-as**
ingl**és**	**-esa**	**-eses**	**-esas**
alem**án**	**-ana**	**-anes**	**-anas**

mand**ón**	**-ona**	**-ones**	**-onas**
hablad**or**	**-ora**	**-ores**	**-oras**

1: (des)cortés has no feminine forms: *una persona (des)cortés*
2: *Bueno→buen, before* masc. sing. nouns: *buen chico,* but *un chico bueno*

Other:
español, español**a**, español**es**, español**as**

b. 2-form Adjectives

Agree with noun only in *number*

Final vowel, masc. sing.:	*-a, -e;* stressed *i, u*
alerta(s)	grande(s)*
inteligente(s)	interesante(s)
iraní(es)	hindú(es)
egoísta(s)	optimista(s)
entusiasta(s)	gris(es)
	feliz, felices

Other: *-or* comparative words:
mayor(es), menor(es), mejor(es), peor(es)

**gran* used before singular nouns: un(a) *gran escritor(a)* but *una casa grande*

c. 1-form Adjectives

Show *no* agreement with noun

claro*	*light*	macho	*male*
extra	*extra*	modelo	*model*
hembra	*female*	oscuro*	*dark*

*When referring to *color* and used with second color adjective, also invariable; compare:

dos coches *verdes*	*two green cars*
dos coches *verde claro*	*two light green cars*

gato(s) macho / hembra

rata(s) macho / hembra

casa(s) modelo

1-10. Noun-Adjective Agreement

Occurs whether noun and adjective are together or separate:

La **chica rubia** se llama María.

La **chica** es **rubia**.

Gender of noun, not biological gender, determines gender of adjective:

Carlos/Julia es una **buena persona**.

María es **rubia**; tiene el pelo **rubio**.

1-11. Position of Adjectives

- **Precede** noun:

"Limiting" adjectives–articles, numbers, most demonstratives, *otro, mucho*, "weak" possessives:

Voy a **la** escuela **los** lunes.

Hay **cien** alumnos en **esa** escuela.

Mi prima vive en la **segunda** casa.

Algunos días no leo **ninguna** revista.

La **otra** maleta contiene **muchas** ropas.

- **Follow** noun:

"Strong" possessives:

un amigo **mío** y dos amigas **tuyas**

Demonstratives in pejorative meaning:

No confío en el tipo **ese**.

I don't trust that guy.

Placement of Descriptive Adjectives

May precede or follow noun:

They **follow** if used to **contrast** members of noun class; in English, these are often *stressed* in speech:

el chico **alto** y el chico **bajo**

*the **tall** boy and the **short** boy*

la cultura **inglesa*** y la cultura **francesa***

***English** culture and **French** culture*

*Adj. of nationality almost always follows noun

They **precede** if not used to distinguish noun from others of same class: proper nouns, "one-of-a-kind"; subjective or emotional responses:

nuestro **sabio** rey *our wise king*

la **hermosa** España *beautiful Spain*

el **maldito** coche	*the darned car*
mi **obstinado** papá	*my stubborn dad*
el **valiente** héroe	*the brave hero*

Compare:

Detesto sus clases **largas** y **aburridas**[1].

Detesto sus **largas** y **aburridas** clases[2].

1: "*I hate his **long, boring** classes.*" (He may also give shorter, more interesting classes.)
2: "*I hate his **long-and-boring** classes.*" (the only kind he gives).

1-12. Adverbs

Adjectives[1] vary; adverbs[2] are **invariable**:

Muchos[1] niños lloran mucho[2].

Los buenos[1] atletas juegan bien[2].

Yo vivo lejos[2]; ellas viven cerca[2].

Adj. + *-mente* = Adj. + *ly*:

-o adjectives: *-o*→*a* + *mente*

rápido→rápidamente

claro→claramente

Others: add *-mente* to singular:

inteligente→inteligentemente

general→generalmente

In series, *-(a)mente* occurs only in last adverb; preceding *-o* words appear in *-a* form, others in singular:

Lo hacen **rápida** y eficientemente.

No se acepta, ni **social** ni políticamente.

1-13. Indefinites and Negatives

algo	something, somewhat
nada	nothing, not at all
alguien	somebody
nadie	nobody
alguno/a(s)[1]	some
ninguno/a[1, 2]	no, none
siempre	always
nunca	never

jamás[3]	never
también	also
tampoco	neither
o...o	either...or
ni...ni	neither...nor

1: *-ún* form used before masc. sing. noun:
¿Hay *algún* (no hay *ningún*) libro?
2: Only singular forms in common use:
¿Hay algunas bananas? No, no hay *ninguna.*
3: Emphatic; less frequent than *nunca*

Double Negatives

When negative follows verb, **no** precedes:

No le digo **nada** a **nadie**.

Nadie viene. / **No** viene **nadie**.

Yo **tampoco** voy. / Yo **no** voy, **tampoco**.

Nunca leemos. / **No** leemos **nunca.**

1-14. Personal Pronouns

a. Subject Pronouns

yo	**nosotros/as**[2]
tú	**vosotros/as**[2, 3]
él/ella/Ud.[1]	**ellos/ellas/Uds.**[4]

1: 3rd-person singular verbs used with these
2: *-as* form used with all-female groups
3: Informal plural *you* form used only in Spain
4: 3rd-person plural verbs used with these

Used for emphasis, clarity; often omitted:

Yo soy profesor; **él** es médico.

Ellos (y no **Uds.**) van conmigo.

Juanito vive aquí; (él) tiene ocho años, (él) va a la escuela y (él) conoce a mi hijita.

THE FOUR *YOU* PRONOUNS
Singular: *tú, Ud. (usted);*
Plural: *vosotros; Uds. (ustedes)*
***tú, vosotros*—informal, take 2nd-person verbs:**
tú: *hablas, comes, vives, eres, etc.*
vosotros: *habláis, coméis, vivís, sois, etc.*
***Ud., Uds.*—formal, share 3rd-person forms:**
Ud. (él, ella): *habla, come, vive...*
Uds. (ellos, ellas): *hablan, comen, viven...*
See also: object pronouns, possessives

b. Direct Object, Indirect Object and Reflexive Pronouns

Three pronoun types that:

- **Are *unstressed***
- **Share 1st and 2nd-person forms:**
  (*me, te, nos, os*)

  The 3rd-person forms differ.

- Immediately precede or follow a verb.
  (see *Pronoun Placement Rules* below)

Direct Object Pronouns

me	**nos**
te	**os**
lo*, la	**los*, las**

**le, les* also used for human masculine dir. obj.

¿**Me** entiendes? Sí, **te** entiendo.

¿Puedes ver**nos**? Sí, puedo ver**los**.

Yo bebo vino. ¿Tú **lo** bebes?

¿Dices que él juega bien? No, no **lo** digo.

Indirect Object Pronouns

me	**nos**
te	**os**
le*	**les***

¿Qué **me** das? **Te** doy el dinero.

¿**Nos** das un dólar? No, **les** doy dos.

Le sirvo café a él; **les** sirvo té a ellas.

**Le, les→se* before direct objects *lo/la/los/las*:
No **le** doy la carta a Juana. No **se la** doy.

Reflexive Pronouns

me	**nos**
te	**os**
se	**se**

¿Cómo **te** llamas? **Me** llamo Luis.

¿**Se** acuestan Uds.? Sí, **nos** acostamos.

No voy a sentar**me**. ¿Vas a sentar**te**?

Pronoun Placement Rules

(Direct, Indirect, Reflexive)

These pronouns *immediately precede*:

- *All* indicative* and subjunctive* verbs:
(*Any person or tense; affirmative or negative)
¿Conoces a Luis / Elena / las chicas?

  Sí, **lo / la / las** conozco.

  No **lo / la / las** he conocido nunca.

  Te enseño, enseñé, etc. la canción.

  Quiero que **te** laves las manos.

- A *negative* imperative:

No **lo** leas.	No **me** critiquéis.
No **le** des la llave.	No **les** hable(n).
No **te** laves.	No **se** lave(n).

These pronouns *follow*:

- A present participle:
¿La manzana? Estoy comiéndo**la**.

  Estábamos lavándo**nos**.

  ¿Estás contándo**le** la historia a Juana?

- An infinitive:
  Me apetece el plato. Voy a probar**lo**.
  Debes pedir**le** ayuda a Pablo.
  Después de lavar**me**, almorcé.

- An *affirmative* imperative:
  La novela es buena. Léa(n)**la**.
  Píde**le** ayuda a Pablo.
  Láva**te** las manos.
  Siéntense **se** Uds.

Pronoun Order in Pairs

- Indirect→Direct:
  Le doy la carta a Luis→**Se la** doy.
  ¿**Me lo** vendes? Sí, **te lo** vendo.

- Reflexive→Indirect:
  A Luisa **se le** ocurre una idea.
  Se nos olvidó el libro.

- Reflexive→Direct:
  Me lavo las manos→**Me las** lavo.
  Si te gusta el suéter, pruéba**telo**.

Pronoun Shifting

In sentences with *conjugated verb + infinitive or participle*, pronoun(s) can be moved leftward with no change in meaning:

¿Vas a comer**lo**?→¿**Lo** vas a comer?

Estoy dándo**sela**.*→**Se la*** estoy dando.

Voy a sentar**me**.→**Me** voy a sentar.

*Pair cannot be split up

c. Prepositional Pronouns

- Same as subject pronouns, except[1]:

mí[1]	**nosotros/as**
ti[1]	**vosotros/as**
él, ella; Ud.; sí[1,3]	**ellos/as; Uds.; sí**[1,3]

[3]reflexive

- Used as above after most prepositions:
  A nosotros y **a ellos** no nos gusta.
  Esto no es **para ella,** es **para él**.
  No sé nada **sobre Uds**.
  ¿Puedes ir **sin mí**?

Exceptions:

Con + mí/ti/sí→conmigo, contigo, consigo

¿Quieres ir **conmigo**? **¿Contigo? ¡Sí!**

Do you want to go with me? With you? Yes!

Pablo trae **consigo** una mochila.

Pablo brings a backpack with him.

yo, tú, used after

entre, menos, excepto, según:

entre *tú* y *yo*   según *tú*

► Neuter pronoun *ello*:

Llueve; por ello, no salimos.

It's raining; due to it (that), we're not going out.

d. Redundant Pronoun Constructions

Prepositional (stressed) pronoun refers to same thing(s) or person(s) as object pronoun; **emphasizes or clarifies.**

► *a* + pronoun←→direct obj. pronoun

No **la** quiero a **ella**; **te** quiero **a ti**.

*I don't love **her**; I love **you**.*

► *a* + (pro)noun←→indirect obj. pronoun

Da**le** el dinero **a Juana**, no **a Julio**.

*Give the money to **Juana**, not to **Julio**.*

A ella no **le** gusta eso, pero a mí sí.

She doesn't like that, but I do.

► With **reflexive** construction:

a sí mismo/a(s) is added for emphasis:

Ella critica a sus amigos; también **se critica a sí misma**.

She criticizes her friends; she also criticizes herself.

► In **reciprocal**, *uno/a(s) a otro/a(s)* is used:

Tú y yo nos ayudamos **uno/a a otro/a**.

You and I help each other.

These eliminate ambiguities in the plural:

Se ayudan **unos a otros,** y **a sí mismos**.

They help each other, and themselves.

Direct object duplication

When direct object* precedes verb, a matching pronoun is inserted:

No comí las uvas.*→Las uvas* no **las** comí.

1-15. "Personal" *a*

Used before direct object (pro)nouns referring to specific persons, or personalized entities.

Visito **a** Pepe y **a** esa chica.

Quiero **a** mi gato.

Muchos critican **a** Hollywood.

¿**A** quién ves? No veo **a** nadie.

Omitted before indefinite persons, after *tener*:

Busco / necesito una **secretaria**.

No tengo **hermanos**.

Clearly marks direct object:

¿Quién llama **a Adán**?

Who calls Adán?

¿**A quién** llama Adán?

Whom does Adán call?

1-16. Possessives

Saying "______'s ______":

el / la / los / las _____ de _____

el libro de Pablo = *Pablo's* book*

las plumas de Juana = *Juana's* pens*

*Spanish *never* uses apostrophe

Ellipsis—noun can be dropped* in series:

la casa de Juana y la * de Pedro

*Juana's house and Pedro's **

Unstressed Possessive Adjectives

mi(s)	*my*	**nuestro/a(s)**	*our*
tu(s)	*your*[1]	**vuestro/a(s)**	*your*[3]
su(s)	*his, her, your*[2]	**su(s)**	*their, your*[4]

1: *tú*
2: *Ud.*
3: *vosotros*
4: *Uds.*

Precede the noun; all agree with noun in number; *nuestro/vuestro* agree in gender:

mi / tu / su hermano/a

mis / tus / sus hermanos(as)

nuestro(s) hermano(s)

vuestra(s) hermana(s)

Clarification of *su*

With no context, *su* is ambiguous:

su libro = *his/her/your/their* book*

sus libros = * *books*

su tía = * *aunt*

sus tías = * *aunts*

To clarify ***su***:

Definite article (***el, la, los, las***) + noun + ***de él/ella/Ud./ellos(as)/Uds.***

su (*his*) libro→el libro **de** él

su (*their*) silla→la silla **de** ellos/as

sus (*your*) tazas→las tazas **de** Ud(s).

Stressed Possessives

mío/a(s)	nuestro/a(s)
tuyo/a(s)	vuestro/a(s)
suyo/a(s)	suyo/a(s)

As **adjectives**, follow noun, agree with it in number and gender:

un amigo/a **mío/a, tuyo/a**, etc.

a friend of mine, yours, etc.

unos/as amigos/as **nuestros/as**

some friends of ours

As **pronouns,** used with definite article:

No uso mi lápiz; uso **el tuyo**.

I don't use my pencil; I use yours.

Yo visito su casa y él visita **la mía**.

I visit his house and he visits mine.

But: Article omitted after *ser*:

Ese vaso no es **tuyo**; es **mío**.

Clarification of *suyo*

Suyo is ambiguous:

Esta pluma es suya.

This pen is his/hers/yours/theirs.

To clarify ***suyo***:

Definite article (***el, la, los, las***) + ***de*** + ***él/ella/Ud./ellos(as)/Uds.***

Él y ella tienen coches; **el de él** es rojo; **el de ella** es verde. (*his is red; hers is green*)

Las chicas y los chicos traen galletas a la fiesta; **las de ellas** son más sabrosas que **las de ellos.**

1-17. Demonstratives

a. Demonstrative Adjectives

this/these

	Masc.	Fem.
Sing.	**este**	**esta**
Pl.	**estos**	**estas**

that/those (near)

	Masc.	Fem.
Sing.	**ese**	**esa**
Pl.	**esos**	**esas**

that/those (remote)

	Masc.	Fem.
Sing.	**aquel**	**aquella**
Pl.	**aquellos**	**aquellas**

esta pera, **ese** queso y **aquellas** bananas

b. Demonstrative Pronouns

this/that one; these/those (ones)

Masc./fem. forms: Same as adjectives, with accents:

éste, ésta, éstos, éstas

ése, ésa, ésos, ésas

aquél, aquélla, aquéllos, aquéllas

esta casa y **ésas**	*this house and those*
este libro y **aquél**	*this book and that one*

Neuter forms: Refer to unidentified objects or to events; no accent used:

esto **eso** **aquello**

Él siempre llega tarde; **eso** no me gusta.

¿Qué es **esto**?

1-18. Interrogatives

¿cómo?	*how?*
¿cuál(es)?	*which?; what?*
¿cuándo?	*when?*
¿cuánto/a(s)?	*how much?; how many?*
¿dónde?	*where?*
¿por qué?	*why?*
¿qué?	*what?; which?*
¿quién(es)?	*who?*

¿Cuál?, ¿quién?, ¿cuánto? agree with noun:

¿**Quién(es)** es/son esa(s) chica(s)?

¿**Cuál** es / **cuáles** son**...?**

¿Cuánto tiempo...? **¿Cuántas horas...?**

***Whose?* = *¿De quién(es)?*:**

¿**De quién** es ese libro?

Whose book is that?

The *¿Qué?/¿Cuál?* Distinction

= *what?, which?*; not interchangeable:

► **Uses of *¿cuál(es)?***

Pronoun: asks listener to choose from a number of possible choices:

¿**Cuál** es tu nombre/teléfono?

What's your name/phone number?

¿**Cuál** es la fecha?

What's the date?

¿**Cuáles** son tus platos favoritos?

What are your favorite dishes?

¿**Cuál(es)** de estas camisas prefieres?

Which of these shirts do you like?

► **Uses of *¿qué?***

As **pronoun**, asks listener to define or identify something:

¿**Qué** es esta cosa? *What's this thing?*

¿**Qué** son «*reptiles*»? *What are "reptiles"?*

Used as **adjective** modifying noun:

¿**Qué** día es? ¿**Qué** deportes practicas?

Tag Questions

(...do you?, didn't he?, etc.)

¿no?; ¿verdad?; ¿no te/le parece?

Es difícil, ¿no? Eres de Perú, ¿verdad?

Eso es ridículo, ¿no te parece?

1-19. Comparisons

a. Comparisons of Inequality

► **más que...** *more than...; -er than...*

► **menos que...** *less (fewer) than...*

Pablo es **más/menos** alto **que** Pedro.

Trabajo **más/menos (horas) que** ellos.

► **De** is used instead of **que** before a number:

Tiene **más/menos *de*** tres hijos.

► **Irregular Comparative Forms**

Positive	**Comparative**
bueno/bien	**mejor**[1]
malo/mal	**peor**[1]

poco	**menos**
mucho	**más**
viejo, grande	**mayor**[1, 2]
joven, pequeño	**menor**[1, 2]

Yo juego bien/mal, pero ellas juegan **mejor/peor** (**que** yo).

Él come mucho, pero yo como **más/menos** (**que** él).

1: Plural (*-es*) form used where applicable:

Ellas son buenas (malas) jugadoras, pero no son las **mejores (peores)**.

2: Regular comparison sometimes used:

Arturo es **mayor / más viejo que** Julio.

¿Son **menores / más jovenes que** yo?

► ***más/menos....del que , de lo que***

Used when 2nd member of comparison is a clause; *de lo que* used to compare adjective[1] or verb[2], *del (de la, de los, de las) que* for a noun[3]:

Es más fácil[1] **de lo que** tú piensas.

It's easier than you think.

Lees[2] menos **de lo que** debes leer.

You read less than you should read.

Hay más postres[3] **de los que** puedo comer.

There are more desserts than I can eat.

Se cultiva más trigo[3] **del que** se consume.

More wheat is grown than is consumed.

b. Comparisons of Equality

(*as...as*)

► **tan + (adj. / adv.) como...**

No soy **tan** inteligente **como** tú.

Ellas son **tan** altas **como** Mario.

¿Entiendes **tan** bien **como** Carlos?

► **(verb) tanto como...**

Ellos comen **tanto como** yo.

Leo mucho, pero no **tanto como** Ud.

- **tanto/a(s) (noun) como...**
  as much / many (noun)...

  No bebo **tanta** leche como Enrique.

  Leo **tantos** libros **como** ellas, pero no **tantos como** él.

> **NOTE:**
> ***Mucho/a(s)* is never used for English *much/many* in comparisons of equality:**
> **Wrong: Leo tanto mucho como él.**
> **Right: Leo tanto como él.**

- ...the same as...

el / la / los / las / lo mismo/a(s)...que...

  Vivo en **la misma** ciudad **que** tú.

  Seguimos **los mismos** cursos **que** ellos.

  Pienso **lo mismo que** mi hermana.

1-20. Prepositions

a. *por* and *para*

> **ABOUT *POR* AND *PARA***
> ***One or the other* fits into a particular context. *They are not generally interchangeable.* The English equivalents vary; see examples below.**

Uses of *por*:

- Inexact location in space or time:
  Trabajo **por** la mañana/tarde/noche.

  Vamos a viajar **por** Francia.

  Por aquí no hay nada que ver.

- *During* a period of time (often omitted):
  Estuve en España (**por**) dos años.

- *In exchange for, instead of*:
  Te doy cinco dólares **por** el libro.

  No puedo ir a clase; ¿puedes ir **por** mí?

- *At the rate of; per*:
  Ramón maneja a cien millas **por** hora.

  Veinte **por** ciento de los chicos faltan.

- *Due to; because of*:
  Mi madre me riñe **por** mi estupidez.

  Por esa razón, decidí quedarme aquí.

- *In support of, in favor of; for the sake of*:
  No voto **por** ese candidato.

  Estoy **por** cancelar la fiesta.

  Sacrifican mucho **por** su país/familia.

- *Through, by means of*:
  No pases **por** esa puerta.

  Vamos **por** tren.

- *By*, meaning agency, authorship, etc.:
  La novela fue escrita **por** Hemingway.

- After *ir*, *venir*, before object of errand:
  Mamá viene **por** mí (*is coming for me*).

  Fui **por** pan y leche.

- Before *adjective* + *que* ("*no matter how...*"):
  Lo haré, **por** difícil que sea.

  I'll do it, no matter how hard it is.

- After some verbs:

acabar por	*wind up (___ing)*
interesarse por	*be interested in*
mirar por	*watch out for*
preguntar por	*inquire about*
preocuparse por (de)	*worry about*
optar por	*opt for*
tomar por	*take for*

  But: *buscar, pedir* take no preposition:

Busco (pido)...	*I look (ask) for...*

- In common idioms:

por ahora	*for now*
por fin	*finally*
¡Por Dios!	*Goodness!*
por lo menos	*at least*
por eso	*therefore*
por supuesto	*of course*

Uses of *para*:

- Use, goal, purpose, object, destination:

  Es una botella **para** leche.

  El regalo es **para** ti.

  Estudio **para** aprender.

  Salimos **para** San Francisco.

  Esta cosa no sirve **para** nada.

  Tenemos comida **para** dos días.

  Trabajamos **para** la universidad.

- (Dis)advantage, perspective:

  Para mí, la química es muy difícil.

  Eso no es bueno **para** la salud.

- *Considering that...*:

  Sabes mucho **para** persona tan joven.

- *By* (a deadline):

  Tengo que terminar todo **para** viernes.

- With *estar, to be about to...**

  Estamos **para** salir.

  Mi suscripción está **para** vencer.

  ***Por** used in Latin America

b. *a, con, de, en*

- **Verb→preposition→Infinitive**

Many verbs take a preposition between themselves and a following infinitive; some take none:

Quiere [ ] salir.	*He wants to leave.*
Me ayudan **a** aprender.	*They help me to learn.*
Sueño **con** volar.	*I dream about flying.*

¡Deja **de** interrumpir!	*Stop interrupting!*
Insiste **en** fumar.	*He insists on smoking.*

► Verb→Preposition→Infnitive Combinations

no preposition

aconsejar	*advise (smb.) to*
conseguir	*manage to*
deber	*should, ought to*
decidir	*decide to*
dejar	*allow, permit (smb.) to*
desear	*want, desire to*
gustar	*be pleasing to*
impedir	*prevent from ___ing*
intentar	*attempt/try to*
lograr	*manage to*
necesitar	*need to*
pensar	*intend to*
poder	*can, be able to*
preferir	*prefer to*
prohibir	*prohibit from ___ing*
prometer	*promise to*
querer	*want to*
resolver	*resolve to*
saber	*know how to*
sentir	*regret ___ing*

Impersonal expressions take no preposition:

Es necesario (importante) entender esto.

It's necessary (important) to understand this.

Hace falta hacer ejercicio.

One ought to exercise.

a

aprender a	*learn to*
atreverse a	*dare to*
ayudar a	*help to*
comenzar a	*begin to*

empezar a	*begin to*
enseñar a	*teach to*
invitar a	*invite to*
ir a	*be going to*
negarse a	*refuse to*
obligar a	*oblige to*
ponerse a	*begin to*
salir a	*go out to*
volver a	*(verb) again*

con

amenazar con	*threaten to*
contar con	*count on*
soñar con	*dream about*

de

acabar de	*have just _____ed*
alegrarse de	*be glad to*
cansarse de	*get tired of ____ing*
deber de	*must (supposition)*
dejar de	*stop ____ing*
jactarse de	*brag about ___ing*
tratar de	*try to*

en

consistir en	*consist of*
dudar en	*hesitate to*
influir en	*influence*
insistir en	*insist on*
quedar en	*agree to*
ser el primero en	*be the first to*

▸ **Verb→Preposition→(Pro)noun**

In many cases English uses no preposition or a different one from Spanish, e.g.:

Asisten **a** la clase. *He attends the class.*

Dependo **de** ellos. *I depend on them.*

► Verb→Preposition→(Pro)noun Combinations

a

asistir a	*attend (class, etc.)*
faltar a	*miss (meeting, etc.)*
jugar al (a la)	*play (sport)*

Sensory verbs:

holer a	*smell like*
parecerse a	*look like*
saber a	*taste like*
sonar a	*sound like*

con

acabar con	*put an end to*
casarse con	*marry (smb.)*
contar con	*count on; have; possess*
soñar con	*dream about*
tratar con	*have dealings with (smb.)*

de

aprovecharse de	*take advantage of*
burlarse de	*make fun of*
cansarse de	*get tired of*
depender de	*depend on*
disfrutar/gozar de	*enjoy*
enamorarse de	*fall in love with*
hacer de	*act as; play the role of*
jactarse de	*brag about*
pensar de	*have an opinion about*
quejarse de	*complain about*
preocuparse de	*worry about*
reírse de	*laugh at*
salir de	*leave from (place)*
tratar de	*be about (subject)*
tratarse de	*be a matter of*

en

consistir en	*consist of*
convertirse en	*convert to; change into*
entrar en	*enter; go into*
pensar en	*think about*

c. Common Compound Prepositions

además de	*besides*	después de	*after*
al lado de	*beside*	detrás de	*behind*
alrededor de	*around*	en vez de	*instead of*
antes de	*before*	encima de	*above*
cerca de	*close to*	enfrente de	*opposite*
debajo de	*under*	frente a	*opposite*
delante de	*in front of*	fuera de	*outside*
dentro de	*inside*	lejos de	*far from*

d. Other Prepositions

ante	*before; faced with*
ante esos problemas	*faced with those problems*
bajo	*under (often fig.)*
bajo su autoridad	*under their authority*
contra	*against*
contra la pared	*against the wall*
desde	*(starting) from*
desde la una hasta...	*from 1:00 until...*
durante	*during; for (time period)*
durante la guerra	*during the war*
durante tres semanas	*for three weeks*
entre	*between; among*
entre la una y las dos	*between 1:00 and 2:00*
entre mis colegas	*among my colleagues*
hacia	*toward; ____ward(s)*
camina hacia la pared	*walk toward the wall*

hasta	*until*
hasta las diez	*until 10:00*
según	*according to*
según tú	*according to you*
sin	*without*
No vayas sin mí.	*Don't go without me.*
sobre	*about; on; above*
sobre todo	*above all*
sobre la mesa	*on (above) the table*
hablar sobre un tema	*speak about a topic*

1-21. *Ser/Estar*

Both mean *to be*; not interchangeable:

Uses of *ser*:

- Identification—(pro)noun = (pro)noun:
  Juan **es** médico. **Somos** mexicanas.

  ¿**Son** tus hijos? **Soy** soldado.

- With adjectives describing **inherent** or **definitive** qualities:
  El béisbol **es** divertido.

  ¿Cómo **es** Adán? **Es** listo y estudioso.

- *To take place* (time or place of event):
  La fiesta **es** en mi casa. **Es** a las dos.

- With *de* meaning *to be from*:
  Somos de Chicago. ¿**De** dónde **eres**?

- With *de* meaning *to be made of*:
  Las corbatas **son de** seda.

- With *de* meaning *to belong to*:
  ¿**De** quién **es** el dinero? **Es de** Pedro.

- In passive before past participle:
  (*to be _____ed [by_____]*)

  Las fórmulas **son** analizadas (por ellos).

  La novela **fue** escrita (por ella).

Uses of *estar*:

- Location of anything physical:
  ¿Dónde **estás**? **Estoy** en Miami.

  Los Andes **están** en Sud América.

- With adjectives / past participles describing conditions that are **non-inherent, atypical** or **the result of an action or change**:
  ¿Cómo **estás**? **Estoy** bien, gracias.

  Tienen un examen y **están** nerviosos.

  ¡Este jugo de naranja **está** agrio! (*sour*)

  Juana, ¡**estás** (*you look*) muy guapa!

  Las ventanas **están** abiertas/cerradas.

  ¿**Están** vivos o muertos sus abuelos?

  Está nublado (*It's cloudy*).

- With present participle in **progressive**:
  ¿Qué **estás** haciendo? **Estoy** leyendo.

1-22. Existential Use of *Haber*

Hay = there is, there are:
¿**Hay** un coche en el garaje? No, **hay** dos.

Other tenses use 3rd-person singular *haber* form before both singular and plural nouns:
Hay un partido hoy. Mañana **habrá** dos.

Hubo un (tres) accidente(s) en esa calle.

Ha habido una (tres) fiesta(s) aquí este mes.

Dudo que **haya** cuatro hijas en esa familia.

1-23. *Saber/Conocer*

= ***to know***; not interchangeable:
saber: possess knowledge, know-how, information:

No **sabemos** (cuál es) su nombre.

¿**Sabes** que él es mi hermano? Sí, lo **sé**.

No **sé** tocar el piano.

In **preterite**, = *found out, learned*:
Ya lo sé. Lo **supe** el viernes.

I already know it. I found (it) out on Friday.

conocer: Be acquainted with (a person, place, etc.):
Yo **conozco** a Juan, pero no sé dónde vive.

¿**Conoces** bien el país / la ciudad?

In **preterite**, = *met for the first time*:
Conozco a José. Lo **conocí** el año pasado.

I know José. I met him last year.

1-24. *Pero/Sino*

= ***but***; not interchangeable:

pero: *however, nevertheless*; used after both affirmative and negative elements; expresses **qualification**:
Luis es listo, **pero** es perezoso.

No puedo ir, **pero** no me importa.

sino: *but rather...*; used only after a negative; what follows **contradicts** what precedes:
Juan no tiene un hermano, **sino** cuatro.

No voy a Francia **sino** a España.

sino que: used to contrast clauses:
No participó activamente, **sino que** pasó todo el día en la cama.

no sólo...sino (que): = *not only...but also*:
No sólo va Juan, **sino** (también) Luis.

No sólo ganó un premio, **sino que** (también) lo invitaron a la Casa Blanca.

1-25. Word Order

In transitive sentences, order is generally like English (Subject[1]→Verb[2]→Object[3]):
Mis padres[1] hablan[2] tres lenguas[3].

Word order is freer than English; **subject** and **verb** are often inverted; this occurs in transitive[1] and intransitive[2] sentences and in subordinate clauses[3].

1: Los **supervisores** me **observan**.
Me **observan** los **supervisores**.
Bell inventó el **teléfono**.
El **teléfono** lo inventó **Bell**.

2: **Llega** el **tren**. **Sale** el **sol**.

3: Eran las tres cuando **José llegó**.
Eran las tres cuando **llegó José**.
Después de que los **niños cenan**...
Después de que **cenan** los **niños**...

A subject[1] with lengthy modifier(s) often follows verb[2]:

Telefoneó[2] hace poco un **señor**[1] que quería hablar con el profesor González.

A gentleman who wanted to talk with Professor González telephoned a while ago.

Word Order in Questions

- *Yes/no* questions:

Subject can precede or follow verb:

¿Tu **tía es** vieja? / **Es** vieja tu **tía**?

¿Su **madre** no **va**? / ¿No **va** su **madre**?

¿**Elsa** te lo **dio**? / ¿Te lo **dio Elsa**?

- Questions with interrogative words:

Subject usually follows verb:

¿Dónde **vive José**?

¿Cómo **están Alicia y Juana**?

¿Cuándo **empieza** la **película**?

¿A qué hora **llegan** los **invitados**?

Note: Spanish uses *verb-subject* order in questions **and** *implied** questions:

¿Qué es eso?

What is that?

*Yo no sé **qué es eso**.

*I don't know **what that is**.*

¿Cómo está su padre?

How is his father?

*Dime cómo **está su padre**.

Tell me how his father is.

1-26. Relative Pronouns

Relative pronouns link two clauses that have a noun in common:

La **niña** es mi hija. La **niña** llora.→La niña **que** llora es mi hija.

Referring to persons or things:

que **el que**[1] **el cual**[2]

1: *el que, la que, los que, las que*
2: *el cual, la cual, los cuales, las cuales*

Referring to persons only: **quien(es)**

► **Que**

The most common; the **only** choice when no comma or preposition precedes:

La ciudad **que** visité fue fascinante.

No conozco al profe **que** da esa clase.

Unlike English, relative cannot be omitted:

Un tipo **que** yo conozco me visitó.

A guy (that) I know visited me.

Can be used after comma or *a, con, de, en*:

Luis, **que** es el tío de Irma, falta hoy.

La persona a **que** me refiero es Carlos.

La casa en **que** vivimos es roja.

► **El que, el cual, quien**

More formal; used after commas, prepositions; sometimes interchangeable:

El edificio, **el que / el cual** compré en 1998, es muy viejo.

Las alumnas **por las que / las cuales / quienes** escribí las cartas se graduaron.

Son personas sobre **quienes / las que / las cuales** no sabemos mucho.

They are persons about whom we don't know much.

► **los/las cuales** used after **algunos/as de**:

Visité muchos museos, algunos de **los cuales** fueron fascinantes.

I visited many museums, some of which were fascinating.

► **El/los/las/que** = ***the one(s) that... B***

Este libro es mejor que *el que* tiene José.

This book is better than the one that José has.

Quiero esas cosas y no *las que* tú quieres.

I want those things, not the ones that you want.

Other Relatives

donde

La ciudad **donde** vivimos está muy lejos.

lo que

Which, what, that which...; neuter: refers to genderless entities, not specific nouns:

Lo que me gusta es que nunca llueve.

What I like is that it never rains.

No entendí **lo que** él me dijo.

I didn't understand what he told me.

lo cual

Used after comma or preposition; interchangeable with **lo que** in those cases:

José no fuma, **lo que / lo cual** es bueno.

José doesn't smoke, which is good.

Llovió, por **lo que / lo cual** no salí.

It rained, and so I didn't go out.

cuyo

Formal possessive adj: = *whose*; agrees with **thing(s) possessed**, not possesor(s):

Te presento a Ana, **cuyo tío** es mi amigo.

This is Ana, whose uncle is my friend.

Conocí al autor **cuyas novelas** había leído.

I met the author whose novels I had read.

Cuyo is not interrogative.

Whose? = ¿De quién(es)...?

1-27. The *Gustar* Structure

Gustar sentences express *(dis)likes*; structure differs from English:

English:	**Spanish:**
I like the book.	"Me pleases the book."
He likes books.	"Him please books."
We like to read.	"Us pleases to read."

► **The basic *gustar* sentence:**

Indirect Object Pronoun + *gusta(n)* + Subject

Me / Te / Le / Nos / Os / Les	1. gusta el libro. 2. gustan los libros. 3. gusta leer y escribir.

I/you/he/she/we/they

1. like the book.

2. like the books.

3. like to read (and write).

¿Te gusta la clase? Sí, me gusta.

Do you like the class? Yes, I like it.

¿Le gustan los huevos? No, no le gustan.

Does she like eggs? No, she doesn't like them.

¿Les gusta nadar? Sí, les gusta.

Do they like to swim? Yes, they like to.

Nos gusta cantar y bailar.*

We like to sing and dance.

*Multiple infinitives take singular verb

► **Expansion: The Redundant «*A*» Phrase**

Adds **emphasis** or **clarification**:

A mí me
A ti te
A él (ella) le
A Ud. le
A Alicia le
A nosotros nos
A Luis y a mí nos
A vosotros os
A ellos (ellas) les
A Uds. les
A las chicas les
A Paco y a Juan les } *

*gusta el libro / gustan los libros / gusta leer.

► Unemphatic→Emphatic:
Me gusta la leche. ¿Te gusta?→

A mí me gusta la leche. ¿**A ti** te gusta?

*I like milk. Do **you** like it?*

► Ambiguous→Clarified:
Le (?) gusta eso, pero no les (?) gusta.→

A él le gusta eso, pero **a ellas** no les gusta.

A is repeated in compound phrases:
A Tomás y **a** mí nos gusta eso. ¿Les gusta **a** ti y **a** Mariana?

«*A*» phrase can be used without verb:
Me gusta el flan. ¿Y **a ti**?

I like flan. And you?

A Juana le gusta. **A nosotros** también.

Juana likes it. So do we.

A Elsa no le gusta. **A Adán**, tampoco.

Elsa doesn't like it. Neither does Adán.

► **Verbs Similar to *Gustar***

encantar	interesar
molestar	caer bien/mal

Nos encanta ir de pesca.

We love to go fishing.

A mis alumnos les interesa la historia.

My students are interested in history.

¿A Uds. les molesta el ruido?

Does the noise bother you?

A Juana no le cae bien Paca.

Juana doesn't like Paca.

1-28. The *-sele* Construction

Describes **unplanned**, often **undesirable**, events that happen to one rather than being one's doing. The structure:

Se **+ Indirect Object Pronoun + 3rd-Person Verb + Subject**

Se { me / te / le / nos / os / les } { 1. olvidó la llave. 2. olvidaron la llaves.

I / you / he / she / we / they

1. forgot the key.

2. forgot the keys.

«*A*» phrase (used as with *gustar*, see 1-27, p. 42):

A Luis se le olvidó la tarea, pero **a mí** no.

Luis forgot the homework, but I didn't.

Other verbs:

Hago el trabajo que **se me asigna**.

I do the work that is assigned to me.

A veces a Pepe **se le ocurren** ideas locas.

Sometimes crazy ideas occur to Pablo.

¡Caramba! ¡**Se me perdió** la billetera!

Darn! My wallet got lost!

Al chico **se le rompió** la pierna.

The boy broke his leg (his leg got broken).

Compare:

Rompí el espejo.

I broke the mirror. (my action)

Se me rompió el espejo.

The mirror"got broken". (It happened to me.)

PART 2: VERB FORMS

Overview of the Spanish Verb System

1. Spanish Verb Tenses and Their English Equivalents (Model English Verb: *talk*)

a. Simple Tenses

Indicative					Subjunctive		Impera-tive	Parti-ciples
Present	Preterite	Imperfect	Future	Condi-tional	Present	Imperfect		
talk(s) *am/is/ are talking* *am/is/are going to talk*	*talked*	*talked* *(used to) talk* *was talking* *was/were going to talk*	*will talk*	*would talk*	...*(that) talk(s)*	...*(that) talked*	*(you) talk!* *let's talk!*	Present: *talking* Past: *talked*

b. Compound Tenses

Indicative				Subjunctive	
Present Perfect	Pluperfect	Future Perfect	Conditional Perfect	Present Perfect	Pluperfect
have/has talked	*had talked*	*will have talked*	*would have talked*	...*(that) have/has talked*	...*(that) had talked*

2. Subject-Verb Agreement in Spanish

In all tenses, Spanish verbs, by their **endings**, show agreement with their **subjects**; in any tense, there are *six* forms, corresponding to these subjects:

1.	*yo*	*I*
2.	*tú*	*you* (singular, informal)
3.	*él/ella; Ud.*	*he; she; it; Elena, the boy, the class,* etc.; *you* (singular, formal)
4.	*nosotros/as*	*we; ___________ and I*
5.	*vosotros/as*	*you* (plural, informal); used only in Spain (Latin America uses *Uds.* instead)
6.	*ellos/ellas; Uds.*	*they; the classes, he and she; Julio and his sister,* etc.; *you* (plural, formal)

Verb conjugations are displayed vertically in the above order on the following pages.

3. Parts of a Verb Form: *Stem* + *Ending*

a. Regular Verb *Stems*

All tenses except future/conditional:	Infinitive **minus** *-ar / -er / -ir*	(EG: ***habl-, com-, viv-***)
Future/conditional:	Infinitive serves as stem:	(EG: ***hablar-, comer-, vivir-***)

b. Regular Verb *Endings*

Regular *-ar* Verbs

Indicative					**Subjunctive**		**Imperative**	**Participles**
Present	Preterite	Imperfect	Future[1]	Conditional[1]	Present	Imperfect		present; past
-o	-é	-aba	-é	-ía	-e	-ara / -ase	—	
-as	-aste	-abas	-ás	-ías	-es	-aras / -ases	-a; no -es	
-a	-ó	-aba	-á	-ía	-e	-ara / -ase	(no) -e	
-amos	-amos	-ábamos	-emos	-íamos	-emos	-áramos /	(no) -emos	
-áis	-asteis	-abais	-éis	-íais	-éis	-ásemos	-ad; no -éis	
-an	-aron	-aban	-án	-ían	-en	-arais /	(no) -en	-ando
						-aseis		
						-aran / -asen		-ado

Regular *-er* and *-ir* Verbs

Indicative					**Subjunctive**		**Imperative**	**Participles**
Present	Preterite	Imperfect	Future[1]	Conditional[1]	Present	Imperfect		present; past
-o	-í	-ía	-é	-ía	-a	-iera / -iese	—	
-es	-iste	-ías	-ás	-ías	-as	-ieras /	-e; no -as	
-e	-ió	-ía	-á	-ía	-a	-ieses	(no) -a	
-emos	-imos	-íamos	-emos	-íamos	-amos	-iera / -iese	(no) -amos	
/	-isteis	-íais	-éis	-íais	-áis	-iéramos /	**-ed / -id**[2];	
-imos[2]	-ieron	-ían	-án	-ían	-an	-iésemos	no -áis	
-éis						-ierais /	(no) -an	
/**-ís**[2]						-ieseis		-iendo
-en						-ieran /		
						-iesen		-ido

1: *Infinitive* used as stem in these tenses
2: *-er* and *-ir* endings differ only in these forms; first ending is for *-er* class, second is for *-ir*

See following pages for full conjugations in all tenses

Spanish Verb Forms: Regular and Irregular, Conjugated in All Tenses

THE SIMPLE TENSES

2-1. Present Indicative

Regular

-ar	-er	-ir
hablar	***comer***	***vivir***
hablo	como	vivo
hablas	comes	vives
habla	come	vive
hablamos	comemos	vivimos
habláis	coméis	vivís
hablan	comen	viven

Stem Changes

► *e→ie* Changes

pensar	***perder***	***mentir***
pienso	**pierdo**	**miento**
piensas	**pierdes**	**mientes**
piensa	**pierde**	**miente**
pensamos	perdemos	mentimos
pensáis	perdéis	mentís
piensan	**pierden**	**mienten**

Other *e→ie* verbs:

See 1b, p. 67

► *o→ue* Changes

contar	***volver***	***morir***
cuento	**vuelvo**	**muero**
cuentas	**vuelves**	**mueres**
cuenta	**vuelve**	**muere**
contamos	volvemos	morimos
contáis	volvéis	morís
cuentan	**vuelven**	**mueren**

Other *o→ue* verbs:

See 1b, p. 67

▸ ***e→i* Changes**

servir	***repetir***
sirvo	**repito**
sirves	**repites**
sirve	**repite**
servimos	repetimos
servís	repetís
sirven	**repiten**

Other *e→i* verbs:

See 1b, p. 67

Irregular in *yo* form only

▸ **c→cz** (*-acer, -ecer, -ocer, -ducir* **verbs):**

nacer	**nazco**
conocer	**conozco**
ofrecer	**ofrezco**
producir	**produzco**

▸ **g insertion (some with other changes):**

caer	**caigo**
poner	**pongo**
hacer	**hago**
salir	**salgo**
traer	**traigo**

▸ **other**

caber	**quepo**
saber	**sé**
dar	**doy**
ver	**veo**

▸ **Consonant Spelling Changes (*yo* only)**

conven***c***er	**conven*z*o**
(*convences, convence,* etc.)	
reco***g***er	**reco*j*o**
(*recoges, recoge,* etc.)	
distin***gu***ir	**distingo**
(*distingues, distingue,* etc.)	

Irregular in more than one form

▸ **Irregular *yo* plus stem changes**

tener	***venir***	***decir***
tengo	**vengo**	**digo**
tienes	vienes	dices
tiene	viene	dice
tenemos	venimos	decimos
tenéis	venís	decís
tienen	vienen	dicen

▸ ***y* insertion: *-uir* verbs; *oír***

concluir	***huir***	***oír***
concluyo	**huyo**	oigo
concluyes	**huyes**	**oyes**
concluye	**huye**	**oye**
concluimos	huimos	oímos
concluís	huís	oís
concluyen	**huyen**	**oyen**

▸ **Other**

estar	***ir***	***haber***	***ser***
estoy	voy	he	soy
estás	vas	has	eres
está	va	ha	es
estamos	vamos	hemos	somos
estáis	vais	habéis	sois
están	van	han	son

Stress Shift

▸ *-iar* verbs: ***enviar*** vs. ***cambiar***

envío	cambio
envías	cambias
envía	cambia
enviamos	cambiamos
enviáis	cambiáis
envían	cambian

Other verbs:

1: variar, esquiar

2: estudiar, limpiar

▸ ***-uar*** **verbs:** ***continuar***[1] **vs.** ***evacuar***[2]

continúo	evacuo
continúas	evacuas
continúa	evacua
continuamos	evacuamos
continuáis	evacuáis
continúan	evacuan

Other verbs :

1: actuar, evaluar

2: averiguar

2-2. Imperatives (Commands)

▸ ***Ud.***

Same as present subjunctive (see 2-7)

(affirmative and negative identical)

hablar	**(no) hable**	sacar	**(no) saque**
comer	**(no) coma**	abrazar	**(no) abrace**
vivir	**(no) viva**	recoger	**(no) recoja**
pensar	**(no) piense**	dar	**(no) dé**
volver	**(no) vuelva**	estar	**(no) esté**

servir	**(no) sirva**	ir	**(no) vaya**
huir	**(no) huya**	saber	**(no) sepa**
llegar	**(no) llegue**	ser	**(no) sea**

► ***Uds.***

Same as present subjunctive , see 2-7, p. 58

(affirmative and negative identical)

All verbs: add *-n* to *Ud.* imperative:

(no) **hablen**, (no) **coman**, (no) **vivan**, etc.

► ***tú* (affirmative)**

Regular:

Same as pres. indic. 3rd-pers. sing. (see 2-1, p. 47)

hablar	**habla**	pensar	**piensa**
comer	**come**	volver	**vuelve**
vivir	**vive**	servir	**sirve**

Irregular:

decir	**di**	salir	**sal**
hacer	**haz**	ser	**sé**
ir	**ve**	tener	**ten**
poner	**pon**	venir	**ven**

► ***tú* (negative)**

Same as present subjunctive (see 2-7, p. 58)

All verbs: add *-s* to *Ud.* imperative

hablar	**no hables**	sacar	**no saques**
comer	**no comas**	abrazar	**no abraces**
vivir	**no vivas**	recoger	**no recojas**
pensar	**no pienses**	dar	**no des**
volver	**no vuelvas**	estar	**no estés**
pedir	**no pidas**	ir	**no vayas**
huir	**no huyas**	ser	**no seas**
llegar	**no llegues**	saber	**no sepas**

▸ ***vosotros*** **(affirmative)**

Non-reflexive, *all* verbs:

Infin. -*r* + *d*

hablar	**hablad**	volver	**volved**
comer	**comed**	pedir	**pedid**
vivir	**vivid**	ser	**sed**
pensar	**pensad**	ir	**id**

Reflexive: *d* dropped

sentarse	**sentaos**
volverse	**volveos**
divertirse	**divertíos**

Exception: irse **idos**

▸ ***vosotros*** **(negative)**

Same as present subjunctive **(see 2-7, p. 58)**

hablar	**no habléis**
comer	**no comáis**
vivir	**no viváis**
pensar	**no penséis**
volver	**no volváis**
pedir	**no pidáis**
huir	**no huyáis**
llegar	**no lleguéis**
sacar	**no saquéis**
abrazar	**no abracéis**
recoger	**no recojáis**
dar	**no deis**
estar	**no estéis**
ir	**no vayáis**
saber	**no sepáis**
ser	**no seáis**

► *Nosotros*

Same as present subjunctive (see 2-7, p. 58)

(affirmative[1] and negative identical[2])

hablar	**(no) hablemos**
comer	**(no) comamos**
vivir	**(no) vivamos**
pensar	**(no) pensemos**
volver	**(no) volvamos**
pedir	**(no) pidamos**
llegar	**(no) lleguemos**
abrazar	**(no) abracemos**
ir	**(no) vayamos**
saber	**(no) sepamos**
ser	**(no) seamos**

1: Affirmative also expressed with *vamos a + infinitive*: **¡Vamos a comer!** ***Let's eat!***
2: In affirmative reflexive, *s* is dropped: **levantémonos**

2-3. Present Participle

► **Regular:**

hablar	**hablando**
comer	**comiendo**
vivir	**viviendo**

► **Stem-changing:** (*e→i; o→u* **in** *-ir* **verbs)**

preferir	**prefiriendo**
servir	**sirviendo**
dormir	**durmiendo**
morir	**muriendo**

► ***i→y*** (*oír; ir; -aer, -eer, -uir* **verbs)**

ir	**yendo**
oír	**oyendo**
creer	**creyendo**
leer	**leyendo**
concluir	**concluyendo**
caer	**cayendo**

► ***i* dropped (-*eír* verbs; stem-final *ñ, ll*)**

reír	**riendo**
reñir	**riñendo**
freír	**friendo**
bullir	**bullendo**

► **Irregular**

poder	**pudiendo**

2-4. Preterite

Regular

-ar	**-er**	**-ir**
hablar	***comer****	***vivir****
hablé	comí	viví
hablaste	comiste	viviste
habló	comió	vivió
hablamos	comimos	vivimos
hablasteis	comisteis	vivisteis
hablaron	comieron	vivieron

*Endings identical in these two classes

Stem Changes

(*e→i; o→u* in *-ir* verbs)

pedir	***preferir***	***dormir****
pedí	preferí	dormí
pediste	preferiste	dormiste
pidió	**prefirió**	**durmió**
pedimos	preferimos	dormimos
pedisteis	preferisteis	dormisteis
pidieron	**prefirieron**	**durmieron**

**dormir, morir* are the only verbs of this type.

Irregular

▸ Irregular stems, common endings

-e, -iste, -o, -imos, -isteis, -ieron

poder	***querer***	***poner***
pude	quise	puse
pudiste	quisiste	pusiste
pudo	quiso	puso
pudimos	quisimos	pusimos
pudisteis	quisisteis	pusisteis
pudieron	quisieron	pusieron

Other stems taking these endings

andar	**anduv-**	producir	**produj-**[1]
caber	**cup-**	reducir	**reduj-**[1]
decir	**dij-**[1]	saber	**sup-**
estar	**estuv-**	tener	**tuv-**
haber	**hub-**	traer	**traj-**[1]
hacer	**hic-**[2]	venir	**vin-**

1. If stem ends in ***j***, 3rd-person plural ending drops ***i***: *dijeron, trajeron*, etc.
2. 3rd-person singular: *hizo*

▸ Other Irregular Verbs

ser/ir	***dar***	***ver***
fui*	di*	vi*
fuiste	diste	viste
fue*	dio*	vio*
fuimos	dimos	vimos
fuisteis	disteis	visteis
fueron	dieron	vieron

*No accents on these forms

▸ **Consonant Spelling Changes**

(*yo* only)

lle*g*ar	**lle*gu*é**
sa*c*ar	**sa*qu*é**
abra*z*ar	**abra*c*é**
averi*gu*ar	**averi*gü*é**

▸ ***i→y* in Third Person**

-aer, -eer, -uir* verbs; *oír

caer	***incluir***	***leer***	***oír***
caí	incluí	leí	oí
caíste	incluiste	leíste	oíste
cayó	**incluyó**	**leyó**	**oyó**
caímos	incluimos	leímos	oímos
caísteis	incluisteis	leísteis	oísteis
cayeron	**incluyeron**	**leyeron**	**oyeron**

▸ ***i* Dropped in 3rd-Person Endings**

(*-eír* verbs; stem-final *ñ, ll*)

reír	***reñir***	***bullir***
reí	reñí	bullí
reíste	reñiste	bulliste
rió	**riñó**	**bulló**
reímos	reñimos	bullimos
reísteis	reñisteis	bullisteis
rieron	**riñeron**	**bulleron**

2-5. Imperfect Indicative

Regular

-ar	**-er***	**-ir***
hablar	***comer***	***vivir***
hablaba	comía	vivía
hablabas	comías	vivías
hablaba	comía	vivía

hablábamos	comíamos	vivíamos
hablabais	comíais	vivíais
hablaban	comían	vivían

*Endings identical in these two classes

Irregular

ir	*ser*	*ver*
iba	era	veía
ibas	eras	veías
iba	era	veía
íbamos	éramos	veíamos
ibais	erais	veíais
iban	eran	veían

2-6. Future/Conditional

Infinitive serves as stem in these tenses

Future endings (*all* verbs):

-é, -ás, -á, -emos, -éis, -án

hablar	*comer*	*vivir*
hablaré	comeré	viviré
hablarás	comerás	vivirás
hablará	comerá	vivirá
hablaremos	comeremos	viviremos
hablaréis	comeréis	viviréis
hablarán	comerán	vivirán

Conditional endings (*all* verbs):

-ía, -ías, -ía, -íamos, -íais, -ían

hablar	*comer*	*vivir*
hablaría	comería	viviría
hablarías	comerías	vivirías
hablaría	comería	viviría
hablaríamos	comeríamos	viviríamos
hablaríais	comeríais	viviríais
hablarían	comerían	vivirían

Irregular Future / Conditional Stems

(*All* verbs use same stem for both tenses)

caber	**cabr-**	querer	**querr-**
decir	**dir-**	saber	**sabr-**
haber	**habr-**	salir	**saldr-**
hacer	**har-**	tener	**tendr-**
poder	**podr-**	valer	**valdr-**
poner	**pondr-**	venir	**vendr-**

2-7. Present Subjunctive

ABOUT PRESENT SUBJUNCTIVE FORMS

Stems: mostly **derived from present indicative *yo* form:**

regular, stem-changing, irregular

Endings: **"*opposite*" vowels from indicative:**

All -ar **verbs have *-e* endings**

All -er **and *-ir*** **verbs have *-a* endings**

Regular

-ar	**-er**	**-ir**
hablar	***comer***	***vivir***
hable	coma	viva
hables	comas	vivas
hable	coma	viva
hablemos	comamos	vivamos
habléis	comáis	viváis
hablen	coman	vivan

Stem Changes

► ***e→ie*** **(*-ar* and *-er* verbs)**

pensar	***entender***
piense	**entienda**
pienses	**entiendas**
piense	**entienda**
pensemos	entendamos
penséis	entendáis
piensen	**entiendan**

► ***o→ue*** **(*-ar* and *-er* verbs)**

contar	***volver***
cuente	**vuelva**
cuentes	**vuelvas**
cuente	**vuelva**
contemos	volvamos
contéis	volváis
cuenten	**vuelvan**

► ***e→ie; e→i*** **(*-ir* verbs)**

sentirse	***preferir***
me sienta	prefiera
te sientas	prefieras
se sienta	prefiera
nos sintamos	prefiramos
os sintáis	prefiráis
se sientan	prefieran

► *e→i* (*-ir* verbs)

servir	***conseguir***
sirva	consiga
sirvas	consigas
sirva	consiga
sirvamos	consigamos
sirváis	consigáis
sirvan	consigan

► ***o→ue; o→u***

(***morir, dormir*** **only**)

morir	***dormir***
muera	duerma
mueras	duermas
muera	duerma
muramos	durmamos
muráis	durmáis
mueran	duerman

Subjunctive from Irregular *yo* form

► **Models**

hacer	***incluir***	***conocer***
(hago)	***(incluyo)***	***(conozco)***
haga	incluya	conozca
hagas	incluyas	conozcas
haga	incluya	conozca
hagamos	incluyamos	conozcamos
hagáis	incluyáis	conozcáis
hagan	incluyan	conozcan

Consonant Spelling Changes

llegar	*distinguir*	*sacar*	*abrazar*
llegue	distinga	saque	abrace
llegues	distingas	saques	abraces
llegue	distinga	saque	abrace
lleguemos	distingamos	saquemos	abracemos
lleguéis	distingáis	saquéis	abracéis
lleguen	distingan	saquen	abracen

vencer	*recoger*	*averiguar*
venza	recoja	averigüe
venzas	recojas	averigües
venza	recoja	averigüe
venzamos	recojamos	averigüemos
venzáis	recojáis	averigüéis
venzan	recojan	averigüen

Irregular Verbs
(*not* derived from *yo* form)

dar	*estar*	*haber*
dé	esté	haya
des	estés	hayas
dé	esté	haya
demos	estemos	hayamos
deis	estéis	hayáis
den	estén	hayan

ir	*saber*	*ser*
vaya	sepa	sea
vayas	sepas	seas
vaya	sepa	sea
vayamos	sepamos	seamos
vayáis	sepáis	seáis
vayan	sepan	sean

2-8. Imperfect Subjunctive

IMPERFECT SUBJUNCTIVE FORMS

Derivation:

From 3rd-person plural form of the preterite, regular and irregular; *no exceptions*:

dar→*dieron*→diera / diese, etc.
hacer→*hicieron*→hiciera / hiciese, etc.
saber→*supieron*→supiera / supiese, etc.

-ra* form is more common than *-se

(-*ra* form)

hablar	***comer***	***vivir***
hablara	comiera	viviera
hablaras	comieras	vivieras
hablara	comiera	viviera
habláramos	comiéramos	viviéramos
hablarais	comierais	vivierais
hablaran	comieran	vivieran

(-*se* form)

hablar	***comer***	***vivir***
hablase	comiese	viviese
hablases	comieses	vivieses
hablase	comiese	viviese
hablásemos	comiésemos	viviésemos
hablaseis	comieseis	vivieseis
hablasen	comiesen	viviesen

ABOUT COMPOUND TENSES

Consist of two parts:

An *haber* form, conjugated in appropriate tense and person

A past participle ending in *-o*

2-9. Past Participle

▸ Regular *-ar*:

Stem + *-ado*	habl|ar	**hablado**

▸ Regular *-er* / *-ir*:

Stem + *-ido*	com|er	**comido**
	viv|ir	**vivido**

▸ Irregular

abrir	**abierto**	leer	**leído***
caer	**caído***	poner	**puesto**
creer	**creído***	reír	**reído***
cubrir	**cubierto**	resolver	**resuelto**
decir	**dicho**	romper	**roto**
describir	**descrito**	satisfacer	**satisfecho**
descubrir	**descubierto**	traer	**traído***
escribir	**escrito**	ver	**visto**
hacer	**hecho**	volver	**vuelto**

*Spelled regularly; accent required

2-10. Present Perfect Indicative

"has / have _____ed"

he
has
ha
hemos
habéis
han
} + past participle

2-11. Pluperfect Indicative

"had _____ed"

había
habías
había
habíamos
habíais
habían
} + past participle

2-12. Future Perfect

"will have _____ed"

habré
habrás
habrá
habremos
habréis
habrán
} + past participle

2-13. Conditional Perfect

"would have _____ed"

habría
habrías
habría
habríamos
habríais
habrían
} + past participle

2-14. Present Perfect Subjunctive

"... that ___ has / have _____ed"

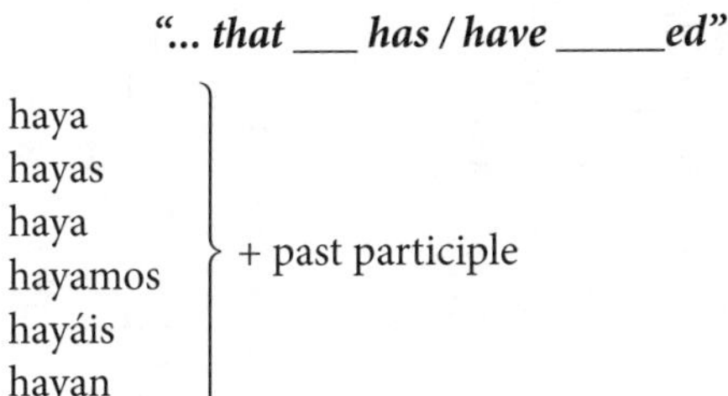

haya
hayas
haya
hayamos
hayáis
hayan
} + past participle

2-15. Pluperfect Subjunctive

"... that ___ had _____ed"

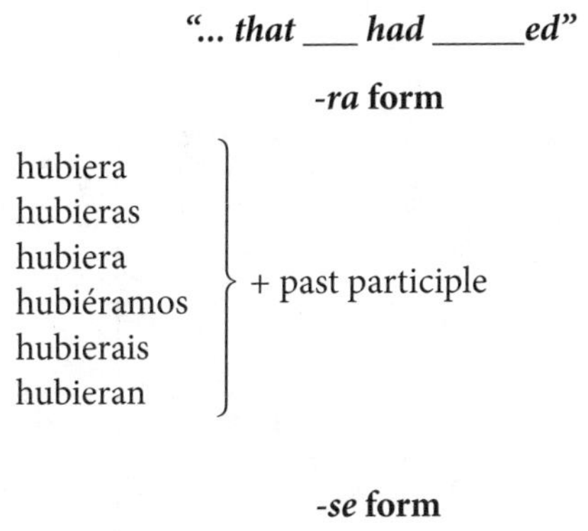

-*ra* form

hubiera
hubieras
hubiera
hubiéramos
hubierais
hubieran
} + past participle

-*se* form

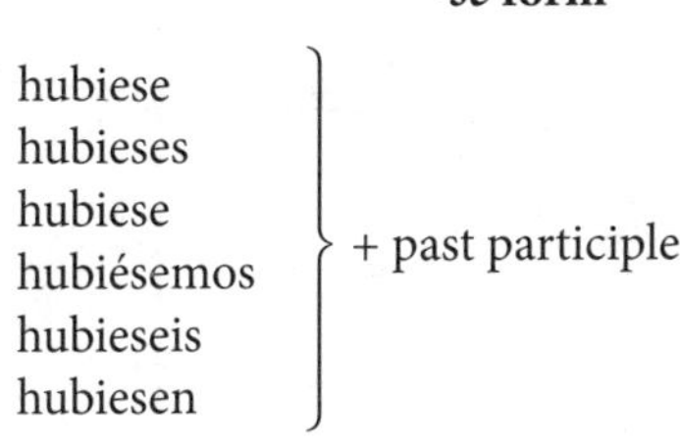

hubiese
hubieses
hubiese
hubiésemos
hubieseis
hubiesen
} + past participle

Irregular Verbs: Lists and Patterns

1. Vowel Stem-Changes

(Affect some verbs whose final stem-vowel is *e* or *o*)

a. Stem-change Patterns: Model Verbs (forms with changes in bold)

TYPE OF CHANGE *INFINITIVE* PRESENT PARTICIPLE PAST PARTICIPLE	INDICATIVE TENSES					SUBJUNCTIVE TENSES		COMMANDS
	PRESENT	PRETERITE	IMPERFECT	FUTURE	CONDITIONAL	PRESENT	IMPERFECT	
1. ie	**pienso**	pensé	pensaba	pensaré	pensaría	**piense**	pensara	—
pensar	**piensas**	pensaste	pensabas	pensarás	pensarías	**pienses**	pensaras	**piensa** / no **pienses**
pensando	**piensa**	pensó	pensaba	pensará	pensaría	**piense**	pensara	(no) **piense** Ud.
pensado	pensamos	pensamos	pensábamos	pensaremos	pensaríamos	pensemos	pensáramos	(no) pensemos
	pensáis	pensasteis	pensabais	pensaréis	pensaríais	penséis	pensarais	pensad / no penséis
	piensan	pensaron	pensaban	pensarán	pensarían	**piensen**	pensaran	(no) **piensen** Uds.
2. ue	**cuento**	conté	contaba	contaré	contaría	**cuente**	contara	—
contar	**cuentas**	contaste	contabas	contarás	contarías	**cuentes**	contaras	**cuenta** / no **cuentes**
contando	**cuenta**	contó	contaba	contará	contaría	**cuente**	contara	(no) **cuente** Ud.
contado	contamos	contamos	contábamos	contaremos	contaríamos	contemos	contáramos	(no) contemos
	contáis	contasteis	contabais	contaréis	contaríais	contéis	contarais	contad / no contéis
	cuentan	contaron	contaban	contarán	contarían	**cuenten**	contaran	(no) **cuenten** Uds.
3. ie, i	**siento**	sentí	sentía	sentiré	sentiría	**sienta**	**sintiera**	—
sentir	**sientes**	sentiste	sentías	sentirás	sentirías	**sientas**	**sintieras**	**siente** / no **sientas**
sintiendo	**siente**	**sintió**	sentía	sentirá	sentiría	**sienta**	**sintiera**	(no) **sienta** Ud.
sentido	sentimos	sentimos	sentíamos	sentiremos	sentiríamos	**sintamos**	**sintiéramos**	(no) **sintamos**
	sentís	sentisteis	sentíais	sentiréis	sentiríais	**sintáis**	**sintierais**	sentid / no **sintáis**
	sienten	**sintieron**	sentían	sentirán	sentirían	**sientan**	**sintieran**	(no) **sientan** Uds.
4. i, i	**pido**	pedí	pedía	pediré	pediría	**pida**	**pidiera**	—
pedir	**pides**	pediste	pedías	pedirás	pedirías	**pidas**	**pidieras**	**pide** / no **pidas**
pidiendo	**pide**	**pidió**	pedía	pedirá	pediría	**pida**	**pidiera**	(no) **pida** Ud.
pedido	pedimos	pedimos	pedíamos	pediremos	pediríamos	**pidamos**	**pidiéramos**	(no) **pidamos**
	pedís	pedisteis	pedíais	pediréis	pediríais	**pidáis**	**pidierais**	pedid / no **pidáis**
	piden	**pidieron**	pedían	pedirán	pedirían	**pidan**	**pidieran**	(no) **pidan** Uds.

5. ue, u	**duermo**	dormí	dormía	dormiré	dormiría	**duerma**	**durmiera**	—
dormir	**duermes**	dormiste	dormías	dormirás	dormirías	**duermas**	**durmieras**	**duerme** / no **duermas**
durmiendo	**duerme**	**durmió**	dormía	dormirá	dormiría	**duerma**	**durmiera**	(no) **duerma** Ud.
dormido	dormimos	dormimos	dormíamos	dormiremos	dormiríamos	**durmamos**	**durmiéramos**	(no) **durmamos**
	dormís	dormisteis	dormíais	dormiréis	dormiríais	**durmáis**	**durmierais**	dormid / no **durmáis**
	duermen	**durmieron**	dormían	dormirán	dormirían	**duerman**	**durmieran**	(no) **duerman** Uds.

b. Some Common Stem-Changing Verbs*

1. *ie*		2. *ue*				
acertar	helar	absolver	jugar (*u*→*ue*)	tostar	invertir	impedir
apretar	manifestar	acordar	llover	tronar	mentir	medir
arrendar	mentar	acostar	moler	volar	preferir	pedir
ascender	merendar	almorzar	morder	volcar	referir	regir
atender	negar	aprobar	mostrar	volver	requerir	reír
atravesar	nevar	avergonzar	mover		sentir	rendir
calentar	pensar	cocer	oler[2]	**3. *ie, i***[3]	sugerir	reñir
cegar	perder	colgar	poder	advertir	transferir	repetir
cerrar	quebrar	comprobar	probar	arrepentirse		seguir
comenzar	querer	contar	promover	asentir	**4. *i, i***[3]	servir
confesar	recomendar	conmover	recordar	consentir	competir	sonreír
defender	sentar	costar	renovar	convertir	concebir	vestir
despertar	temblar	demostrar	resolver	diferir	conseguir	
empezar	tender	desaprobar	rodar	digerir	corregir	**5. *ue, u***
encender	tener[1]	descontar	rogar	divertir	derretir	dormir
encerrar	tentar	devolver	soler	herir	despedir	morir
entender	trascender	disolver	soltar	hervir	desvestir	
enterrar	tropezar	encontrar	sonar	ingerir	elegir	
fregar	venir[1]	esforzar	soñar	interferir	freír	
gobernar	verter	forzar	torcer			

*Some verbs with stem-final *e* or *o* but no stem change: *aceptar, aprender, beber, comer, comprar, comprender, correr, cortar, coser, meter, montar, ofender, vender*

1. These verbs (and their compounds) have additional irregularities, and do not have the full paradigm of changes shown in **1a** tables.
See **Present Indicative (2-1), Present Subjunctive (2-7), Preterite (2-4)**

2. Forms with stem-change spelled with initial *h*: *huele, huela*, etc.

3. *Almost* all *-ir* verbs whose final stem-vowel is *e* have the *e*→*i* changes shown in patterns **3** and **4** (see **1a** tables); *sumergir* (*sumergió*, etc.) is one exception.
Reflexive Verbs: Stem-changes also occur if verb is used reflexively: *acostar(se)*→*(me) acuesto*, etc.

2. Patterns in Consonant Spelling Changes

What these changes are and how they work:

- Spelling of consonant sound at **end of verb stem** is affected: sa**c**ar; abra**z**ar; lle**g**ar; averi**gu**ar; reco**g**er, etc.
- Spelling varies depending on the following vowel sound; **pronunciation** of consonant remains the same
- Spelling changes are in accord with **General Rules of Spanish Spelling**
- In all cases the consonant sound is spelled one way before *a, o*, another way before *e, i*

Spelling of Consonant Sounds, as Determined by Following Vowel

[k]		[s][1] ([th])[2]		[g]		[gw]		*jota*[4]	
ca co	que[3] qui[3]	za zo	ce ci	ga go	gue[3] gui[3]	gua guo	güe güi	ja jo	ge gi
saca saco	saque delinquí	abraza abrazo venzo venza	vence vencí	llega llego siga sigo	sigue siguió seguí	averigua averiguo argua arguo	argüe averigüe argüí	recoja recojo	recoge recogí

1. Spelling of *letter s* does not vary: pasa, paso, pase
2. Pronunciation used in Spain
3. «*u*» in *que, qui, gue, gui* is silent
4. In *-jar, -jer* verbs, «*j*» spelling maintained throughout: arro*j*a, arro*j*e; te*j*e; te*j*a

3. Some Common Verbs With Irregular Present-Tense *yo* Forms (Stem of Present Subjunctive)

caber	**quepo**	incluir	**incluyo**	reducir	**reduzco**
caer	**caigo**	influir	**influyo**	salir	**salgo**
conducir	**conduzco**[1]	introducir	**introduzco**	satisfacer	**satisfago**
conocer	**conozco**	merecer	**merezco**	tener	**tengo**
construir	**construyo**[2]	nacer	**nazco**	traducir	**traduzco**
crecer	**crezco**	obedecer	**obedezco**	traer	**traigo**

decir	**digo**	ofrecer	**ofrezco**	valer	**valgo**
destruir	**destruyo**	oír	**oigo**	venir	**vengo**
establecer	**establezco**	parecer	**parezco**	ver	**veo**
hacer	**hago**	poner	**pongo**		
huir	**huyo**	producir	**produzco**		

1. *-acer, -ecer, -ocer, -ducir* verbs have *c→zc* change: (exception: *cocer→cuezo*)
2. *-uir* verbs insert *y*

4. Compounds of Common Irregular Verbs

a. RULE: These have the same irregular forms as their root verbs; some examples follow:

1) Present indicative *yo* forms→Present Subjunctive:

de**caer**	de**caigo**→de**caiga**	a**parecer**	a**parezco**→a**parezca**	pre**venir**	pre**vengo**→pre**venga**
des**conocer**	des**conozco**→des**conozca**	o**poner**	o**pongo**→o**ponga**	des**hacer**	des**hago**→des**haga**
pre**decir**	pre**digo**→pre**diga**	man**tener**	man**tengo**→man**tenga**	a**traer**	a**traigo**→a**traiga**

2) Stem changes:
en**cerrar** (en**cierr**-) de**volver** (de**vuelv**-) pre**sentir** (pre**sient**-, pre**sint**-) im**pedir** (im**pid**-)

3) Affirmative *tú* imperatives
su**poner** (su**pón**) rehacer (re**haz**) man**tener** (man**tén**)

4) Preterite:
re**hacer** re**hice**, etc. pro**poner** pro**puse**, etc. re**tener** re**tuve**, etc. pre**venir** pre**vine**, etc.

5) Future/Conditional Stems:
re**poner** (re**pondr**-) re**tener** (re**tendr**-) des**hacer** (des**har**-)

6) Past participles:
des**hacer** (des**hecho**) o**poner** (o**puesto**) re**volver** (re**vuelto**)

b. Exceptions:

1) All compounds of *decir* are regular in affirmative *tú* imperative[a], future/conditional[b]
   a **predice, maldice, etc.** b **predeciré / predeciría; maldeciré / maldeciría**, etc.

2) *bendecir* and *maldecir* (but not the other *-decir* verbs) are regular in the past participle:
   bendecido, maldecido But: desdicho, contradicho, predicho

5. Complete Conjugations of Common Irregular Verbs (Irregular Forms in Bold)

INFINITIVE PRESENT PARTICIPLE PAST PARTICIPLE	INDICATIVE TENSES					SUBJUNCTIVE TENSES		IMPERATIVES
	PRESENT	PRETERITE	IMPERFECT	FUTURE	CONDITIONAL	PRESENT	IMPERFECT	
andar	ando	**anduve**	andaba	andaré	andaría	ande	**anduviera**	—
andando	andas	**anduviste**	andabas	andarás	andarías	andes	**anduvieras**	anda / no andes
andado	anda	**anduvo**	andaba	andará	andaría	ande	**anduviera**	(no) ande Ud.
	andamos	**anduvisteis**	andábamos	andaremos	andaríamos	andemos	**anduviéramos**	(no) andemos
	andáis	**anduvimos**	andabais	andaréis	andaríais	andéis	**anduvierais**	andad / no andéis
	andan	**anduvieron**	andaban	andarán	andarían	anden	**anduvieran**	(no) anden Uds.
caer	**caigo**	caí	caía	caeré	caería	**caiga**	**cayera**	—
cayendo	caes	caíste	caías	caerás	caerías	**caigas**	**cayeras**	cae / no **caigas**
caído	cae	**cayó**	caía	caerá	caería	**caiga**	**cayera**	(no) **caiga** Ud.
	caemos	caímos	caíamos	caeremos	caeríamos	**caigamos**	**cayéramos**	(no) **caigamos**
	caéis	caísteis	caíais	caeréis	caeríais	**caigáis**	**cayerais**	caed / no **caigáis**
	caen	**cayeron**	caían	caerán	caerían	**caigan**	**cayeran**	(no) **caigan** Uds.
dar	**doy**	**di**	daba	daré	daría	dé	**diera**	—
dando	das	**diste**	dabas	darás	darías	des	**dieras**	da / no des
dado	da	**dio**	daba	dará	daría	dé	**diera**	(no) dé Ud.
	damos	**dimos**	dábamos	daremos	daríamos	demos	**diéramos**	(no) demos
	dais	**disteis**	dabais	daréis	daríais	deis	**dierais**	dad / no deis
	dan	**dieron**	daban	darán	darían	den	**dieran**	(no) den Uds.

decir	**digo**	**dije**	decía	**diré**	**diría**	**diga**	**dijera**	—
dicho	**dices**	**dijiste**	decías	**dirás**	**dirías**	**digas**	**dijeras**	**di** / no **digas**
diciendo	**dice**	**dijo**	decía	**dirá**	**diría**	**diga**	**dijera**	(no) **diga** Ud.
	decimos	**dijimos**	decíamos	**diremos**	**diríamos**	**digamos**	**dijéramos**	(no) **digamos**
	decís	**dijisteis**	decíais	**diréis**	**diríais**	**digáis**	**dijerais**	decid / no **digáis**
	dicen	**dijeron**	decían	**dirán**	**dirían**	**digan**	**dijeran**	(no) **digan** Uds.
estar	**estoy**	**estuve**	estaba	estaré	estaría	**esté**	**estuviera**	—
estado	**estás**	**estuviste**	estabas	estarás	estarías	**estés**	**estuvieras**	**está / no estés**
estando	**está**	**estuvo**	estaba	estará	estaría	**esté**	**estuviera**	(no) **esté Ud.**
	estamos	**estuvimos**	estábamos	estaremos	estaríamos	estemos	**estuviéramos**	(no) **estemos**
	estáis	**estuvisteis**	estabais	estaréis	estaríais	estéis	**estuvierais**	estad / no **estéis**
	están	**estuvieron**	estaban	estarán	estarían	**estén**	**estuvieran**	(no) **estén Uds.**
haber	**he**	**hube**	había	**habré**	**habría**	**haya**	**hubiera**	
habido	**has**	**hubiste**	habías	**habrás**	**habrías**	**hayas**	**hubieras**	
habiendo	**ha**	**hubo**	había	**habrá**	**habría**	**haya**	**hubiera**	
	hemos	**hubimos**	habíamos	**habremos**	**habríamos**	**hayamos**	**hubiéramos**	
	habéis	**hubisteis**	habíais	**habréis**	**habríais**	**hayáis**	**hubierais**	
	han	**hubieron**	habían	**habrán**	**habrían**	**hayan**	**hubieran**	
hacer	**hago**	**hice**	hacía	**haré**	**haría**	**haga**	**hiciera**	—
haciendo	haces	**hiciste**	hacías	**harás**	**harías**	**hagas**	**hicieras**	**haz** / no **hagas**
hecho	hace	**hizo**	hacía	**hará**	**haría**	**hag**	**hiciera**	(no) **haga** Ud.
	hacemos	**hicimos**	hacíamos	**haremos**	**haríamos**	**hagamos**	**hiciéramos**	(no) **hagamos**
	hacéis	**hicisteis**	hacíais	**haréis**	**haríais**	**hagáis**	**hicierais**	haced / no **hagáis**
	hacen	**hicieron**	hacían	**harán**	**harían**	**hagan**	**hicieran**	(no) **hagan** Uds.
incluir	**incluyo**	incluí	incluía	incluiré	incluiría	**incluya**	**incluyera**	—
incluyendo	**incluyes**	incluiste	incluías	incluirás	incluirías	**incluyas**	**incluyeras**	**incluye** / no **incluyas**
incluido	**incluye**	**incluyó**	incluía	incluirá	incluiría	**incluya**	**incluyera**	(no) **incluya** Ud.
	incluimos	incluimos	incluíamos	incluiremos	incluiríamos	**incluyamos**	**incluyéramos**	(no) **incluyamos**
	incluís	incluisteis	incluíais	incluiréis	incluiríais	**incluyáis**	**incluyerais**	incluid / no **incluyáis**
	incluyen	**incluyeron**	incluían	incluirán	incluirían	**incluyan**	**incluyeran**	(no) **incluyan** Uds.

INFINITIVE PRESENT PARTICIPLE PAST PARTICIPLE	INDICATIVE TENSES					SUBJUNCTIVE TENSES		IMPERATIVES
	PRESENT	PRETERITE	IMPERFECT	FUTURE	CONDITIONAL	PRESENT	IMPERFECT	
ir	**voy**	**fui**	**iba**	iré	iría	**vaya**	**fuera**	—
yendo	**vas**	**fuiste**	**ibas**	irás	irías	**vayas**	**fueras**	**ve** / no **vayas**
ido	**va**	**fue**	**iba**	irá	iría	**vaya**	**fuera**	(no) **vaya** Ud.
	vamos	**fuimos**	**íbamos**	iremos	iríamos	**vayamos**	**fuéramos**	(no) **vayamos**
	vais	**fuisteis**	**ibais**	iréis	iríais	**vayáis**	**fuerais**	id / no **vayáis**
	van	**fueron**	**iban**	irán	irían	**vayan**	**fueran**	(no) **vayan** Uds.
oír	**oigo**	oí	oía	oiré	oiría	**oiga**	**oyera**	—
oyendo	**oyes**	oíste	oías	oirás	oirías	**oigas**	**oyeras**	**oye** / no **oigas**
oído	**oye**	**oyó**	oía	oirá	oiría	**oiga**	**oyera**	(no) **oiga** Ud.
	oímos	oímos	oíamos	oiremos	oiríamos	**oigamos**	**oyéramos**	(no) **oigamos**
	oís	oísteis	oíais	oiréis	oiríais	**oigáis**	**oyerais**	oíd / no **oigáis**
	oyen	**oyeron**	oían	oirán	oirían	**oigan**	**oyeran**	(no) **oigan** Uds.
poder	**puedo**	**pude**	podía	**podré**	**podría**	**pueda**	**pudiera**	
pudiendo	**puedes**	**pudiste**	podías	**podrás**	**podrías**	**puedas**	**pudieras**	
podido	**puede**	**pudo**	podía	**podrá**	**podría**	**pueda**	**pudiera**	
	podemos	**pudimos**	podíamos	**podremos**	**podríamos**	podamos	**pudiéramos**	
	podéis	**pudisteis**	podíais	**podréis**	**podríais**	podáis	**pudierais**	
	pueden	**pudieron**	podían	**podrán**	**podrían**	**puedan**	**pudieran**	
poner	**pongo**	**puse**	ponía	**pondré**	**pondría**	**ponga**	**pusiera**	—
poniendo	pones	**pusiste**	ponías	**pondrás**	**pondrías**	**pongas**	**pusieras**	**pon** / no **pongas**
puesto	pone	**puso**	ponía	**pondrá**	**pondría**	**ponga**	**pusiera**	(no) **ponga** Ud.
	ponemos	**pusimos**	poníamos	**pondremos**	**pondríamos**	**pongamos**	**pusiéramos**	(no) **pongamos**
	ponéis	**pusisteis**	poníais	**pondréis**	**pondríais**	**pongáis**	**pusierais**	poned / no **pongáis**
	ponen	**pusieron**	ponían	**pondrán**	**pondrían**	**pongan**	**pusieran**	(no) **pongan** Uds.
querer	**quiero**	**quise**	quería	**querré**	**querría**	**quiera**	**quisiera**	—
queriendo	**quieres**	**quisiste**	querías	**querrás**	**querrías**	**quieras**	**quisieras**	**quiere** / no **quieras**
querido	**quiere**	**quiso**	quería	**querrá**	**querría**	**quiera**	**quisiera**	(no) **quiera** Ud.
	queremos	**quisimos**	queríamos	**querremos**	**querríamos**	queramos	**quisiéramos**	(no) queramos
	queréis	**quisisteis**	queríais	**querréis**	**querríais**	queráis	**quisierais**	quered / no queráis
	quieren	**quisieron**	querían	**querrán**	**querrían**	**quieran**	**quisieran**	(no) **quieran** Uds.

saber	**sé**	**supe**	sabía	**sabré**	**sabría**	**sepa**	**supiera**	—
sabiendo	sabes	**supiste**	sabías	**sabrás**	**sabrías**	**sepas**	**supieras**	sabe / no **sepas**
sabido	sabe	**supo**	sabía	**sabrá**	**sabría**	**sepa**	**supiera**	(no) **sepa** Ud.
	sabemos	**supimos**	sabíamos	**sabremos**	**sabríamos**	**sepamos**	**supiéramos**	(no) **sepamos**
	sabéis	**supisteis**	sabíais	**sabréis**	**sabríais**	**sepáis**	**supierais**	sabed / no **sepáis**
	saben	**supieron**	sabían	**sabrán**	**sabrían**	**sepan**	**supieran**	(no) **sepan** Uds.
salir	**salgo**	salí	salía	**saldré**	**saldría**	**salga**	saliera	—
saliendo	sales	saliste	salías	**saldrás**	**saldrías**	**salgas**	salieras	**sal** / no **salgas**
salido	sale	salió	salía	**saldrá**	**saldría**	**salga**	saliera	(no) **salga** Ud.
	salimos	salimos	salíamos	**saldremos**	**saldríamos**	**salgamos**	saliéramos	(no) **salgamos**
	salís	salisteis	salíais	**saldréis**	**saldríais**	**salgáis**	salierais	salid / no **salgáis**
	salen	salieron	salían	**saldrán**	**saldrían**	**salgan**	salieran	(no) **salgan** Uds.
ser	**soy**	**fui**	**era**	seré	sería	**sea**	**fuera**	—
siendo	**eres**	**fuiste**	**eras**	serás	serías	**seas**	**fueras**	**sé** / no **seas**
sido	**es**	**fue**	**era**	será	sería	**sea**	**fuera**	(no) **sea** Ud.
	somos	**fuimos**	**éramos**	seremos	seríamos	**seamos**	**fuéramos**	(no) **seamos**
	sois	**fuisteis**	**erais**	seréis	seríais	**seáis**	**fuerais**	sed / no **seáis**
	son	**fueron**	**eran**	serán	serían	**sean**	**fueran**	(no) **sean** Uds.
tener	**tengo**	**tuve**	tenía	**tendré**	**tendría**	**tenga**	**tuviera**	—
teniendo	**tienes**	**tuviste**	tenías	**tendrás**	**tendrías**	**tengas**	**tuvieras**	**ten** / no **tengas**
tenido	**tiene**	**tuvo**	tenía	**tendrá**	**tendría**	**tenga**	**tuviera**	(no) **tenga** Ud.
	tenemos	**tuvimos**	teníamos	**tendremos**	**tendríamos**	**tengamos**	**tuviéramos**	(no) **tengamos**
	tenéis	**tuvisteis**	teníais	**tendréis**	**tendríais**	**tengáis**	**tuvierais**	tened / no **tengáis**
	tienen	**tuvieron**	tenían	**tendrán**	**tendrían**	**tengan**	**tuvieran**	(no) **tengan** Uds.
traer	**traigo**	**traje**	traía	traeré	traería	**traiga**	**trajera**	—
trayendo	traes	**trajiste**	traías	traerás	traerías	**traigas**	**trajeras**	trae / no **traigas**
traído	trae	**trajo**	traía	traerá	traería	**traiga**	**trajera**	(no) **traiga** Ud.
	traemos	**trajimos**	traíamos	traeremos	traeríamos	**traigamos**	**trajéramos**	(no) **traigamos**
	traéis	**trajisteis**	traíais	traeréis	traeríais	**traigáis**	**trajerais**	traed / no **traigáis**
	traen	**trajeron**	traían	traerán	traerían	**traigan**	**trajeran**	(no) **traigan** Uds.

INFINITIVE PRESENT PARTICIPLE PAST PARTICIPLE	INDICATIVE TENSES					SUBJUNCTIVE TENSES		IMPERATIVES
	PRESENT	PRETERITE	IMPERFECT	FUTURE	CONDITIONAL	PRESENT	IMPERFECT	
venir	**vengo**	**vine**	venía	**vendré**	**vendría**	**venga**	**viniera**	—
viniendo	**vienes**	**viniste**	venías	**vendrás**	**vendrías**	**vengas**	**vinieras**	**ven** / no **vengas**
venido	**viene**	**vino**	venía	**vendrá**	**vendría**	**venga**	**viniera**	(no) **venga** Ud.
	venimos	**vinimos**	veníamos	**vendremos**	**vendríamos**	**vengamos**	**viniéramos**	(no) **vengamos**
	venís	**vinisteis**	veníais	**vendréis**	**vendríais**	**vengáis**	**vinierais**	venid / no **vengáis**
	vienen	**vinieron**	venían	**vendrán**	**vendrían**	**vengan**	**vinieran**	(no) **vengan** Uds.
ver	**veo**	vi	**veía**	veré	vería	**vea**	viera	—
viendo	ves	viste	**veías**	verás	verías	**veas**	vieras	ve / no **veas**
visto	ve	vio	**veía**	verá	vería	**vea**	viera	(no) **vea** Ud.
	vemos	vimos	**veíamos**	veremos	veríamos	**veamos**	viéramos	(no) **veamos**
	veis	visteis	**veíais**	veréis	veríais	**veáis**	vierais	ved / no **veáis**
	ven	vieron	**veían**	verán	verían	**vean**	vieran	(no) **vean** Uds.

PART 3: USES OF THE VERB TENSES

3-1. Present Indicative

- "Timeless" present–actions or states that habitually occur or are true:

Escribe y **habla** francés.	*He writes and speaks French.*
No **nieva** mucho en la Florida.	*It doesn't snow much in Florida.*
Tokio **es** la capital de Japón.	*Tokyo is the capital of Japan.*

- Future intent:

Salgo el viernes.	*I'm leaving (going to leave) Friday.*
¿Con quién **se casa** Claudia?	*Whom is Claudia going to marry?*
¿**Vas** a nadar hoy?	*Are you going to swim today?*

- Progressive; actions occurring as one speaks:

Escuchamos música (ahora).	*We're listening to music (now).*
¿Con quién **hablas**?	*With whom are you speaking?*

- Imperative (less abrupt than a command form):

Me **llamas** a las dos, ¿vale?	*Call me at two, ok?*
Nos **trae** los menús, por favor.	*Bring us the menus, please.*

- Equivalent of 1st-person questions *should (shall) I/we...?*

¿**Estudio** los verbos?	*Should (Shall) I study the verbs?*
¿**Entramos** ahora?	*Should (Shall) we go in now?*

- Informal recounting of a past episode (historical present):

  Después, **entro** y **veo** que nadie **está** allí.

  Then, I go (went) in and I see (saw) that nobody is (was) there.

3-2. The Present Participle

Invariable, always ending in *-o*

Uses *with* an auxiliary verb:

- After *estar* to form the **progressive**:

Están (estaban) **viendo** la tele.	*They are (were) watching TV.*
Voy a estar **trabajando** allí.	*I'm going to be working there.*

- After verbs of motion *andar, entrar, ir, salir* to describe ongoing events:

Vamos **conociéndo**nos.	*We are getting to know each other.*
Los niños entraron **gritando**.	*The kids came in yelling.*
Anda **molestando** a los demás.	*He goes around bothering others.*
El ladrón salió **corriendo**.	*The thief took off running.*

- After *seguir, continuar* to mean *keep on ______ing*:

  Siguen (continúan) **hablando**. *They keep on talking.*

- After *acabar* to mean *wind up ______ing*:

  Acabé **perdiendo** dinero. *I wound up losing money.*

- After verbs of perception:

Vi a José **bailando** con Juana.	*I saw José dancing with Juana.*
Si te oigo **riñendo** a Carlos...	*If I hear you scolding Carlos...*

- After *llevar + time expression (= have/had been ______ing)*:

  ¿Cuánto tiempo llevas / llevabas **estudiando** español?

  How long have / had you been studying Spanish?

Uses *without* an auxiliary verb:

- *"(by)______ing"; since / inasmuch as / in order to ______:*

  Lo terminamos **trabajando** día y noche.

  We finished it by working day and night.

  Viendo que era inútil, salimos.

  Seeing (since we saw) that it was useless, we left.

  Siendo eso el caso, no hay remedio.

  That being (since that is) the case, it can't be helped.

  Me escribió **pidiendo** dinero.

  She wrote me asking for (in order to ask for) money.

Present participle is **not** used:

To express future intent:

I'm leaving soon = Salgo pronto. See **Present Indicative**, pp. 47, 75

After prepositions:

without speaking = sin hablar See **Infinitive**, p. 77

As a noun:

Seeing is believing = Ver es creer. See **Infinitive**, p. 77

As an adjective*†:

people working here = personas que trabajan aquí

*Some equivalents of *-ing* adjectives:
interesante (*interesting*), anglohablante (*English-speaking*), divertido (*amusing*), crema de afeitar (*shaving cream*), coche comedor (*dining car*)

†Exceptions: **hirviendo** (hervir) and **ardiendo** (arder) are used as adjectives

3-3. Imperatives (Commands)

▸ ***tú, Ud., vosotros, Uds.***

Used to instruct or order one or more persons to do or *not* do something:

tú:	**habla** español	**no hables** inglés
Ud.	**póngase** los zapatos	**no se ponga** las sandalias
vosotros	**comed** las manzanas	**no comáis** los postres
Uds.	**vayan** con ellos	**no vayan** con ella

Subject pronoun, when expressed, follows verb:

Piense **Ud.** / piensen **Uds.** en eso.	*Think about that.*
No quiero hacerlo. ¡Hazlo **tú**!	*I don't want to do it.* ***You*** *do it!*

▸ ***Nosotros—let's (not) + verb***

Affirmative—Present subjunctive or *Vamos a + infinitive*:

Leamos / vamos a leer tres capítulos.	*Let's read three chapters.*
Sentémonos aquí.	*Let's sit here.*

Negative—Present subjunctive

No leamos esa novela.	*Let's not read that novel.*
No nos sentemos aquí.	*Let's not sit here.*

See **Present Indicative**, **Infinitive**, **Future** for other types of commands

3-4. The Infinitive

Used as a **noun** in the following functions:

▸ Completer to a variety of verbs, as subject[1] or object[2]:

No nos gusta **almorzar**[1] aquí.	*We don't like to eat lunch here.*
No quiero **ir**[2].	*I don't want to go.*
¿Prefieren Uds. **comer**[2] a las dos?	*Do you prefer to eat at two?*

▸ Object of preposition:

Sueño con **estudiar** en París.	*I dream about studying in Paris.*
No salgas sin **comer** primero.	*Don't leave without eating first.*
Se estudia para **aprender**.	*One studies in order to learn.*
Lo riñen por **llegar** tarde.	*They scold him for arriving late.*

- Translates English use of *-ing* as noun, sometimes with article:

  Ver es **creer**. — *Seeing is believing.*

  (El) **correr** es divertido. — *Running is fun.*

- Used as a command in instructions and signs:

  Elegir una pregunta y **contestar** usando oraciones completas.

  Choose one question and answer using complete sentences.

  No **fumar**. — *No smoking.*

- Used after **al** to mean *when / on / upon ___ing*:

  Al **llegar**, lo telefoneamos.

  When we arrived (upon arriving), we phoned him.

  Al **ver** a la reina, los señores se descubrieron.

  On seeing the queen, the gentlemen removed their hats.

- After *llevar + time expression + sin* to indicate time during which an event has / had *not* occurred:

  Llevamos/llevábamos siete años sin **ver** a nuestra hermana.

  We haven't/hadn't seen our sister in seven years.

- After verbs of perception:

  ¿Quieres oírme **tocar**? — *Do you want to hear me play?*

  No vi **salir** a tus amigos. — *I didn't see your friends leave.*

- Used even in presence of subject to make the action more abstract:

  ¿Yo **beber** whiskey? ¡Ni **soñar**!

  Me drink whiskey? Don't even think (dream) about it!

3-5. The Preterite/Imperfect Distinction (P/I)

- **P** and **I** are two simple (one-word) past-tense verb conjugations.
- The **P/I** distinction has no consistent counterpart in English; English equivalents are not generally reliable as a guide.
- In speaking of a past event, speaker chooses **P** or **I** depending on speaker's **focus point** on the event—its **beginning, middle or end**.
- If one is substituted one for the other in a given context, this changes the focus point. **P** and **I** are not simply interchangeable. See rules and examples below.

a. The Preterite

1. Actions or states that were **complete** at speaker's focus point:

    Estuvimos en Cuba durante una semana.

    We were in Cuba for a week.

    ¿Por qué **pediste** ese plato?

    Why did you order that dish?

P is often used to recount a **sequence** of single complete events:

Marta **fue** a la panadería, **compró** pan, **pagó** y **volvió** a casa.

Marta went to the bakery, bought bread, paid and returned home.

2. Actions or states that **began** at speaker's focus point:

    Al oír las noticias, todos **gritaron/aplaudieron/lloraron**.

    On hearing the news, everybody (began to) yell/clap/cry.

    Almorcé a las doce y **descansé** a la una.

    I had lunch (beginning) at twelve, and rested (beginning) at one.

b. The Imperfect

1. Actions habitually performed, states that were generally true:

    Cuando **era** niño no me **gustaba** el frío; nunca **salía** en invierno.

    When I was a child I didn't like the cold; I never went out in winter.

    La chica **se llamaba** Mariana. **Era** alta y delgada. Se **parecía** mucho a mi prima. Frecuentemente **llevaba** una sudadera roja en la que **estaba** escrito el nombre de la universidad donde ella **estudiaba**. **Vivía** en un pueblo que **se encontraba** muy cerca de mi ciudad natal.

    The girl was called Mariana. She was tall and slender. She looked a lot like my cousin. She often wore a red sweatshirt on which the name of the university where she studied was written. She lived in a town that was very close to my hometown.

2. Events that were **in progress** at speaker's focus point:

    Eran las tres de la tarde. Mamá **bañaba** al bebé, Pablito **lloraba** porque nadie le **prestaba** atención, Ana y yo **escribíamos** algo para una clase, y Papá **miraba** un partido en la tele.

    It was three in the afternoon. Mom was bathing the baby, Pablito was crying because nobody was paying any attention to him, Ana and I were writing something for a class, and Dad was watching a game on TV.

3. Ongoing past intent; anticipated events:

    Iba a contarle esa historia.

    I was going to tell him that story.

    Si ese profesor no me **aceptaba**, (yo) no **venía** a esta universidad.

    If that teacher wasn't going to accept me, I wasn't going to come to this university.

c. Applications: Combining the Preterite and the Imperfect

- One event (**P**) occurs as another (**I**) is in progress:

  Dormía cuando sonó el teléfono.

  I was sleeping when the phone rang.

  Le pregunté cómo se llamaba.

  I asked him what his name was.

  Eran las nueve cuando me levanté.

  It was nine o'clock when I got up.

  ¿Cuántos años tenías cuando te casaste?

  How old were you when you got married?

- **P** and **I** are often combined in narrating past events. **P**[1] has the effect of pulling the story forward (telling "what happened"); **I**[2] provides background to the events, characters involved.

  Eran[2] las tres y media cuando **llegué**[1] a casa. Al llegar, **vi**[1] que la puerta **estaba**[2] abierta. **Me pregunté**[1] por qué **era**[2] así. De repente, **llegaron**[1] mi hijo y su amigo. **Reñí**[1] a mi hijo, que normalmente no **se olvidaba**[2] de tales cosas, por haber salido de casa sin cerrar la puerta. **Se disculpó**[1] y **prometió**[1] tener más cuidado.

  It was three o'clock when I got home. On arriving, I saw that the door was open. I wondered why that was so. Suddenly, my son and his friend arrived. I scolded my son, who normally didn't forget such things, for having left without locking the door. He apologized and promised to be more careful.

d. Using P or I to Show Different Focus Points on Same Event

Sample event: Juan **cenar**.

P: Juan **cenó** con nosotros ayer. (single completed event)

Juan **cenó** ayer a las siete. (event began at 7:00)

I: Juan **cenaba** aquí mucho cuando era alumno. (habitual)

Juan **cenaba** cuando sonó el teléfono. (event in progress)

Juan dijo que no **cenaba/iba a cenar** porque estaba ocupado. (intent)

e. Differences in English Equivalents to P and I

In some cases, certain verbs are translated with one English verb when used in **P**, and another when used in **I**; these are applications of the above rules, and are **not exceptions** or **special cases**. They point up lexical differences between English and Spanish.

conocer **Conocimos** (*met for the first time*) a Juana recientemente. Antes, no la **conocíamos** (*did not know her).*

saber **Supe** (*I found out*) hoy que él es mexicano. No lo **sabía** *(did not know it*).

querer	**Quise** (*I tried*) explicarle eso a Paco, pero él no **quiso** (*refused to*) escucharme. **Quería** (*he wanted to*) hablar de otras cosas.
tener	**Tuve** (*I obtained*) otra copia de esa novela. Ya **tenía** (*already possessed*) tres copias.

3-6. The Future

- Expresses strong intent:

  Si quieres que lo haga, lo **haré**. — *If you want me to do it, I'll do it.*

  ¡Venceremos! — *We shall overcome!*

Often interchangeable with present; present is more common when emphasis is not needed:

  Te veo / veré mañana. — *I'll see you tomorrow.*

- Speculation about a present event:

  Su abuelo **tendrá** unos noventa años, ¿no?

  His grandfather would be about ninety years old, wouldn't he?

  ¿Por qué **pensarán** así?

  Why (I wonder) do they think that way?

- Very emphatic commands:

  ¡No **saldrás**! ¡**Te quedarás** en casa y **harás** tu tarea!

  *You will **not** go out! You will stay home and do the chores!*

  ¡No **matarás**! — *Thou shalt not kill!*

3-7. The Conditional

- What would happen under certain expressed or implied conditions:

  ¡Nunca le **diría** eso! — *I would never tell him that!*

  ¿**Irías** a París si pudieras? — *Would you go to Paris if you could?*

- Speculation about a past event:

  Sería una persona generosa. — *He must have been a generous person.*

  Ese día **haríamos** diez escalas. — *That day we must have made ten stops.*

- Serves as past equivalent to the future in "backshifted" sentences:

  Dice que no irá a París→Dijo que no **iría** a París.

  He says he won't go to Paris→He said he wouldn't go to Paris.

- Used in polite requests; sounds softer than present or imperative:

  ¿**Podrías** ayudarme? — *Could you help me?*

  ¿**Tendría** Ud. tiempo para hacerlo? — *Would you have time to do it?*

3-8. The Reflexive Construction

The Spanish reflexive is used much more than in English, and in many cases is reflexive in **form** but not in **meaning**.

- **"True" reflexive**—subject acts on itself:

Me llamo Adán.	*I call myself (my name is) Adán.*
¿Cuándo **te levantas**?	*When do you get (yourself) up?*
Hay que **analizarse**.	*One must analyze oneself.*

  Reciprocal (plural only: subjects act on each other)

Elena y yo **nos vemos**.	*Elena and I see each other.*
No **se critiquen** Uds.	*Don't criticize each other.*

Note: To avoid confusion, reflexive and reciprocal can be clarified:

- Reciprocal: **uno/a(s) a otro/a(s)**
  Reflexive: **a sí mismo/a(s)**
  EG: Juan y Paco se curan.

Se curan **uno a otro**.	*They cure each other.*
Se curan **a sí mismos**.	*They cure themselves.*

- Many verbs occur in reflexive to describe emotional states or changes:
  EG: sentirse, encontrarse, ponerse, alegrarse, aburrirse

¿Cómo **te sientes / te encuentras**?	*How do you feel?*
Me siento / me encuentro mal.	*I feel bad.*
Julia **se pone** furiosa cuando yo...	*Julia gets furious when I...*
Nos aburrimos si no podemos salir.	*We get bored if we can't go out.*

- Many actions of grooming and daily routine are expressed reflexively:
  EG: cepillarse, lavarse, bañarse, vestirse

Pablito, **lávate** las manos.	*Pablito, wash your hands.*
Me cepillo después de **vestirme**.	*I brush my hair after dressing.*

- A few common verbs are always reflexive in form:
  atreverse (a) *to dare to*

No **me atrevo** a tomar ese examen.	*I don't dare to take that test.*

  jactarse (de) *to brag (about)*

No **te jactes** de tus notas.	*Don't brag about your grades.*

  quejarse (de) *to complain (about)*

Nos quejamos del trabajo.	*We complain about the work.*

Compare: **Reflexive** (R) vs. **Non-Reflexive** (NR):

Me pongo (R) furiosa al oír eso. Eso siempre me pone (NR) furiosa.

I get furious when I hear that. That always makes me furious.

Me lavo (R) el pelo, y después le lavo (NR) el pelo a Mariana.

I wash my hair, and then I wash Mariana's hair.

3-9. Non-Reflexive Uses of *se*

- **Impersonal *se*:** *"One" + verb*; 3rd-person singular only; used with intransitive verbs and those with a personal direct object preceded by *a*:

  Allí **se vive** muy bien; no **se ve** a muchos pobres.

  One lives very well there; one doesn't see many poor people.

  Si **se viaja** mucho, **se debe** usar cheques de viajero.

  If one travels a lot, one should use traveler's checks.

Note: *tú* and *ellos* forms are also used impersonally in a *non*-reflexive construction; subject pronouns are omitted:

A veces **tienes** que aceptar las consecuencias.

Sometimes you have (one has) to accept the consequences.

Dicen que «*el uso hace maestro*».

They say "practice makes perfect".

- **Passive *se*:** 3rd-person singular or plural, subject agrees with verb, may preceed or follow it; the agent is not expressed.

  Donde **se alquilan** coches **se aceptan** tarjetas de crédito.

  Wherever cars are rented, credit cards are accepted.

  Allí **se factura** el equipaje y **se confirma** la reservación.

  There, the baggage is checked and the reservation is confirmed.

3-10. The Perfect Indicative Tenses

a. Present Perfect

- Indicates completion of event as of present time, often within the current time period (day, month, etc.); sometimes refers to life experience:

  Vi a González ayer, pero no lo **he visto** hoy.

  I saw González yesterday, but I haven't seen him today.

  ¿**Has probado** alguna vez ese plato?

  Have you ever tried that dish?

Note: The simple present is used with *hace* for events extending from a point in past through the present:

Hace tres años que **vivo** aquí. *I've lived here for three years.*

b. Pluperfect (Past Perfect)

Indicates completion of event as of a reference point in past:

Probé ese postre anoche. Nunca lo **había probado** antes.

I tried that dessert last night. I had never tried it before.

Ya **nos habíamos acostado** cuando sonó el teléfono.

We had already gone to bed when the phone rang.

Note: Imperfect is used with *hacía* for event extending from remote past to nearer past:

Encontré a Julia en el centro ayer. **Hacía** un año que no la **veía**.

I ran into Julia in town yesterday. I hadn't see her for a year.

c. Future Perfect

- Predicts completion of event as of a reference point in the future:

  Ya **habremos salido** cuando Uds. lleguen.

  We will have already left when you arrive.

  En 2020, ya **me habré jubilado**.

  In 2020, I will have already retired.

- Speculates about completion of events as of the present:

  ¿Cuántas veces me **habrá contado** esa historia?

  How many times do you suppose he's told me that story?

d. Conditional Perfect

- States what would have happened under certain conditions, expressed or implied:

  En ese caso, no les **habría dicho** nada.

  In that case, I wouldn't have told them anything.

  Si les hubieras pedido ayuda, con mucho gusto te **habrían ayudado**.

  If you had asked them for help, they'd have gladly helped you.

- Speculates about the completion of past events:

  El **habría cometido** quince delitos antes de que lo prendieran.

  He'd probably committed fifteen offenses before they arrested him.

Note: Pluperfect subjunctive is often used as conditional perfect:

Si hubiera salido a las tres, **hubiera (habría) llegado** a tiempo.

If I'd left at three, I would have arrived on time.

3-11. The Variable Past Participle

The variable *(-o, -a, -os, -as)* past participle is an adjective (and sometimes a noun) that occurs in a variety of structures.

a. Use as Adjective or Noun

Participle often acts as adjective[1], becomes noun[2] with use of article:

No como nunca huevos **revueltos**[1]; prefiero **los cocidos**[2].

I never eat scrambled eggs; I prefer hard-boiled (ones).

Es una persona muy **dedicada**[1].

S/he's a very dedicated person.

¡Qué **divertido/entretenido**[1]!

What fun! How entertaining!

Sabemos los nombres de **los muertos**[2] y **los heridos**[2].

We know the names of the dead and the wounded.

b. The *ser* Passive

Subject **undergoes action**; agent* sometimes expressed:

Mi artículo **fue discutido** (por esa clase*).

My article was discussed (by that class).

¿Por quién* **fueron escritas** esas cartas?

By whom were those letters written?

c. Use with *estar*

Subject is in a **state** that is a **result** of an action performed on it:

Los exámenes **están corregidos**. Yo los corregí.

The exams are corrected. I corrected them.

Cuando llegamos, el puente ya estaba destruido.

When we arrived, the bridge was already destroyed.

d. Use with *Tener*

¿Los exámenes? Sí, ya los **tengo corregidos**.

The exams? Yes, I already have them corrected.

Ya **teníamos leídas** veinte páginas cuando ella llamó.

We already had thirty pages read when she called.

e. "Absolute" Construction

A formal structure used instead of a clause:

Terminadas (después de que terminaron) las clases, nos fuimos.

The classes having ended, we left.

Resuelto (si se resolviera) ese problema, podríamos descansar.

If that problem were solved, we could rest.

3-12. The Subjunctive/Indicative (S/I) Distinction

- **Subjunctive** and **Indicative** are two of the three **moods** that verbs are used in; the third is the **Imperative** (commands: See Section 3-3.)
- There are nine indicative tenses (five simple, four compound) and four subjunctive tenses (two simple, two compound) in common use today.
- The **subjunctive** is most commonly used in subordinate (dependent) clauses, when certain elements in the main clause trigger it; it has some uses in main clauses as well.

a. The Subjunctive and Indicative in Noun Clauses

- The **indicative*** is used in a noun clause if the main clause contains a statement of **affirmation, belief**, etc.:

  Es verdad (obvio, cierto) que tú **eres*** el mejor candidato.

  Supongo que los padres de Raúl no **hablan*** inglés.

  Juana cree que el examen **es*** fácil.

  Nos parece que todos **van*** a la fiesta el sábado.

  El presidente declara que no **está*** de acuerdo con los senadores.

- The **subjunctive*** is used in a noun clause if the main clause contains one of three "triggers":

1) **An attempt to influence** (also called "volition"):

   No quiero que mis hijos **escuchen*** esa música.

   I don't want my kids to listen to that music.

Recomendamos que tú no **salgas*** por la noche en esa ciudad.

We recommend that you don't go out at night in that city.

Es necesario que ellos **hagan*** la tarea antes de ver la tele.

It's necessary that they do their homework before watching TV.

El profe me pide que lo **ayude*** después de la clase.

The prof asks me to help him after class.

Te sugiero que no **fumes*** aquí.

I suggest that you not smoke here.

Other verbs that show an attempt to influence:

aconsejar, dejar, desear, exigir, mandar, preferir

Verbs of communication: *decir, insistir en, sugerir, escribir:*

These take **S** if there's an attempt to influence, **I** otherwise:

Le digo a Pablo que **se ponga** el abrigo. Le digo que **hace** frío.

I tell Pablo to put on his coat. I tell (inform) him that it's cold.

Juana me sugiere que **estudie**. Eso sugiere que le **importan** mis notas.

Juana suggests that I study. That suggests that my grades matter to her.

Insistimos en que no **vayan**. Ellos insisten en que no **hay** peligro.

We insist that they not go. They insist (maintain) that there's no danger.

Escríbele que **venga** a las tres, y que **cenamos** a las cuatro.

Write to him telling him to come at three, and that we're eating at four.

2) An emotional reaction or value judgment:

Es bueno que Uds. **puedan** hablar español.

It's good that you speak Spanish.

Nos irrita que el profe siempre **llegue** tarde.

It irritates us that the prof always arrives late.

Me alegro de que ellos **quieran** ir a Chicago con nosotros.

I'm glad that they want to go to Chicago with us.

3) Doubt, denial, uncertainty, (im)possibility, (im)probability:

No creemos que ella **sea** la mejor jugadora del equipo.

We don't think that she's the best player on the team.

Dudo que Pablo **vuelva** pronto.

I doubt that Pablo will return soon.

Ellas no están seguras de que Manolo las **entienda**.

They're not sure that Manolo understands them.

Es posible que **me ponga** muy nervioso durante el examen.

It's possible that I'll get very nervous during the test.

In some **questions**, **S/I** choice depends on speaker's belief:

¿Crees que **es** posible?

Do you believe it's possible (as I do)?

¿Crees que **sea** posible?

Do you believe it's possible (I have my doubts)?

b. The Subjunctive and Indicative in Adjective Clauses

- The **indicative** is used in an adjective clause if the clause refers to an **antecedent*** whose existence is affirmed:

  Tengo un amigo* que **corre** diez kilómetros al día.

  I have a friend that runs ten kilometers a day.

  Conozco a muchas personas* que **participan** en la política.

  I know many people that participate in politics.

  Hay muchos libros* que **contienen** esa información.

  There are a lot of books that contain that information.

- The **subjunctive** is used if the clause refers to an **antecedent*** whose existence or identity is uncertain or whose existence is denied:

  ¿Tienes un amigo* que **corra** diez kilómetros al día?

  Do you have a friend that runs ten kilometers a day?

  Busco / quiero un **coche*** que **cueste** menos de dos mil.

  I am looking for (want) a car that costs less than two thousand.

  Cualquier alumno* que **necesite** ayuda debe telefonearme.

  Any student who needs help should phone me.

  No tengo ningún amigo* que **corra** diez kilómetros al día.

  I don't have a friend that runs ten kilometers a day.

  No hay nadie* aquí que **participe** en la política.

  There's no one here that participates in politics.

c. Sequence of Tenses in Subjunctive-Requiring Situations

Choice of subjunctive tense in the subordinate clause is determined by the tense of the main clause verb. There are two **sequences, present** and **past.**

1) Present Sequence

Main Clause Verb	Subordinate Clause Verb
imperative; present or future	present (perfect) subjunctive

Examples:

No conozco / he conocido a nadie que **hable** chino.

I don't know / have not known anyone who speaks Chinese.

Dígales a los chicos que **dejen** de gritar.

Tell the boys to stop screaming.

La fiesta termina / terminará antes de que **lleguemos**.

The party ends / will end before we arrive.

A Luis no le gusta / ha gustado que (yo) **fume**.

Luis does not like / has not liked the fact that I smoke.

Present perfect subjunctive is used if event precedes that of main verb:

No conozco a nadie que **haya estudiado** chino.

I don't know anyone who has studied Chinese.

2) Past Sequence

Main Clause Verb	Subordinate Clause Verb
any past or conditional tense	imperfect or pluperfect subjunctive

Examples:

Me alegré / alegraba de que todos **supieran** montar a caballo.

I was glad that everyone knew how to ride a horse.

En esa situación, le pediría a Tomás que me **ayudara**.

In that situation, I'd ask Tomás to help me.

Pluperfect subjunctive is used if event precedes that of main verb:

Necesité / necesitaba un empleado que ya **se hubiera graduado**.

I needed an employee who had already graduated.

d. Adverbial Clauses (1): S/I After Time Conjunctions

Cuando Clauses: A Pattern for Many Time Clauses

Verb after *cuando* is **I** if event is *realized*—known to occur or have occurred:

Cuando **llegan**, les sirvo una taza de café.

When they arrive, I serve them a cup of coffee.

Cuando **llegaron (llegaban)**, les serví / servía una taza de café.

When they arrived, I served (used to serve) them a cup of coffee.

S is used if event is or was still in the future:

Cuando **lleguen**, les voy a servir una taza de café.

When they arrive, I'm going to serve them a cup of coffee.

Cuando **llegaran**, les iba a servir una taza de café.

When they arrived, I was going to serve them a cup of coffee.

Other time words that take **S** or **I** as in the **"*cuando*" pattern** above:

a medida que (*as*); **después (de) que** (*after*); **en cuanto** (*as soon as*); **hasta que** (*until*); **mientras (que)** (*while*); **siempre que** (*as soon as, whenever*); **tan pronto como** (*as soon as*)

Hago los quehaceres mientras el bebé **duerme**.

I do the chores while the baby sleeps.

Enseñé hasta que **sonó** la campana.

I taught until the bell rang.

Tan pronto como **terminen / hayan terminado** de cenar, vengan a verme.

As soon as you finish / have finished eating supper, come see me.

Jorge pensaba tocar el piano hasta que yo **volviera / hubiera vuelto** a casa.

Jorge intended to play the piano until I returned / had returned home.

Exception: ***antes (de) que*** always takes **S**, even with realized events:

Siempre me levanto antes de que **suene** el despertador.

I always get up before the alarm goes off.

Siempre me levantaba antes de que **sonara** el despertador.

I always got up before the alarm went off.

e. Adverbial Clauses (2): S/I After Non-Time Conjunctions

▸ ***puesto que, ya que, en vista de que, debido a que*** express certainty, take **I**:

Puesto que / ya que no **voy** de vacaciones, no necesito hacer la maleta.

Since I'm not going on vacation, I don't need to pack.

En vista de que / debido a que **nieva**, nos quedamos en casa.

In view of / due to the fact that it's snowing, we're staying home.

▸ **Conjunctions of Cause, Condition** or **Purpose** take **S**:

Usa un micrófono para que todos **puedan** oír.

He uses a microphone so that all can hear.

¿Puedes salir sin que tus amigos lo **sepan**?

Can you go out without your friends knowing it?

Te permito sentarte aquí con tal (de) que no me **molestes**.

I'll let you sit here provided that you don't bother me.

Other conjunctions of this type:

a menos que (*unless*); **a condición de que** (*on the condition that*); **a fin de que** (*so that*); **con tal (de) que** (*provided that*); **en caso de que** (*in case*); **para que** (*in order that, so that*); **sin que** (*without*)

▸ ***de modo que / de manera que***

These take **I** when what follows is the **result** of the preceding action:

El profe lo explica bien, de modo que todos **entienden**.

The prof explains it well, and so (as a result) everybody understands.

Mi esposo escondió las llaves, de manera que no **pude** encontrarlas.

My husband hid the keys, and as a result I couldn't find them.

▸ They take **S** when what follows is the **purpose** or **intent** of the action:

El profe lo explica bien, de modo que todos **entiendan**.

The prof explains it well, so (in order) that everybody will understand.

Mi esposo escondió las llaves, de manera que el bebé no **pudiera** encontrarlas.

My husband hid the keys, so that the baby couldn't find them.

► **Conjunctions of Concession:** ***a pesar de que / aunque / aun cuando***

S is used after these to express doubt about what follows; **I** otherwise:

Aunque no **es / sea** la solución ideal, es aceptable.

Although it isn't / might not be the ideal solution, it's acceptable.

A pesar de que él **era / fuera** el mejor candidato, no voté por él.

In spite of the fact that he was / might have been the best candidate, I didn't vote for him.

► ***por + adjective/adverb...*** (*= no matter how...*)

S is used if event is (was) not realized:

Voy a escuchar el discurso, por aburrido que **sea**.

I'm going to listen to the speech, no matter how boring it is.

Por bien que **juegues**, no ganarás a ésos.

No matter how well you play, you won't beat those guys.

Creíamos poder resolverlo, por difícil que **fuera**.

We thought we could solve it no matter how difficult it was.

With realized events, **I** is used:

Por mucho que se **esfuerza**, nunca llega a tiempo.

No matter how hard he tries, he never arrives on time.

Por mucho que lo **busqué**, no pude encontrar el documento.

No matter how much I looked, I couldn't find the document.

f. The Subjunctive in Indirect Commands

An **indirect command** is a *que* clause in which speaker expresses a wish that an action be performed by other person(s); English uses *may, let, have*:

No quiero lavar los platos; que los **lave** Pablo.

I don't want to wash the dishes; let (have) Pablo wash them.

¿Que no les gusta el vino? ¡Que **beban** agua, entonces!

They don't like the wine? Let them drink water, then!

Que is omitted in certain fixed expressions:

Dios te **bendiga**, hijo.	*May God bless you, my son.*
Haya luz.	*Let there be light.*

A *que*-structure can be used with other persons to express a wish:

¡**Que** lo pases bien!	*(I hope you) Have a good time!*

g. Subjunctive and Indicative in *si*- Clauses

A number of **S** and **I** tenses are used in *si*-clauses:

- **Present indicative**: "timeless" present statement or prediction about **future**:

  Si **se estudia**, se sale bien en los exámenes.

  If one studies, one does well on exams.

  Si **sales** ahora, llegarás a tiempo.

  If you leave now, you will arrive on time.

- **Imperfect subjunctive**: **speculation** about future event *or* statement that is **contrary to present fact**; conditional used in main clause:

  Si **salieras** ahora, llegarías a tiempo.

  If you left now, you would arrive on time.

  Si **tuviera** más dinero, saldría a comer frecuentemente.

  If I had more money, I'd go out to eat frequently.

- **Pluperfect subjunctive: contrary to past fact**; conditional perfect or conditional used in main clause:

  Eso no habría pasado si me **hubieras** escuchado.

  That wouldn't have happened if you had listened to me.

  Si **hubiéramos invertido** dinero en esa empresa, seríamos millonarios.

  If we'd invested money in that company, we'd be millionaires.

- **Indicative past tense**:

1) Statements that main clause in fact followed from *si*-clause:

   Si yo **salía** de la casa, mi hermanito siempre me seguía.

   If I went out of the house, my little brother always followed me.

   Si **se estudiaba**, se salía bien en los exámenes.

   If one studied, one did well on exams.

2) Speaker accepts (at least temporarily) that *si*-clause is true, then states what follows from it, or questions it:

   Si Juana te **dijo** eso, lo puedes creer.

   If Juana told you that, you can believe it.

   Si el martes **fue** el quince, (entonces) hoy es el diecisiete.

   If Tuesday was the fifteenth, then today is the seventeenth.

   Si **jugabas** tan bien, ¿por qué siempre perdías?

   If you played so well, why did you always lose?

Si no **había estudiado**, ¿por qué estaba tan relajado antes del examen?

If (as he says) he hadn't studied, why was he so relaxed before the exam?

como si... *(as if; as though)*
Followed by **imperfect subjunctive** or **pluperfect subjunctive**

Actúa como si él **fuera** el líder del grupo.

He acts as though he were the leader of the group.

Me contestó como si no **hubiera oído** ni una sola palabra.

He answered me as if he had not heard a single word.

h. The Subjunctive in Simple (Single-Clause) Sentences

- After ***quizá(s), tal vez, acaso,*** etc.
  S is used to express greater degree of doubt, **I** a lesser degree:

  Quizás/tal vez/acaso **vienen / vengan** a las dos.

  Perhaps they will come at 2:00.

  No sé quién hizo eso. Quizás/tal vez/acaso lo **hizo/hiciera** Pablo.

  I don't know who did that. Perhaps Pablo did it.

- After ***ojalá***
  Ojalá (*would that...; God grant that...*) always takes the subjunctive; it can be followed by *que*. It expresses hopes or wishes.

  Followed by **present** or **present perfect subjunctive** = *Espero que...*

  Ojalá (que) **tengamos** dinero suficiente para ir a Hawaii.

  I hope we have enough money to go to Hawaii.

  Ojalá (que) nadie me **haya oído** decir eso.

  I hope nobody heard me say that.

  Followed by **imperfect** or **pluperfect subjunctive** = *I wish...*; expresses wishes that are contrary to present or past fact.

  Ojalá (que) **tuviéramos** más dinero.

  I wish we had more money.

  Ojalá (que) el presidente **hubiera visitado** a nuestra ciudad.

  I wish the president had visited our city.

i. *Forma Reduplicativa*

A subjunctive verb form is repeated in dependent clause, offering alternatives.

- Relative pronoun used between verbs (= ____*ever, no matter*, etc.)

  Sean cuales sean las razones, esto no es aceptable.

  Whatever the reasons are, this is not acceptable.

  Venga quien venga a la fiesta, yo no pienso venir.

  I don't intend to come to the party regardless of who is coming.

  Vayamos donde vayamos, la situación será similar.

  Wherever we go, the situación will be similar.

  Sea cuando sea la boda, todos iremos.

  Whenever (no matter when) the wedding is, we'll all go.

  Quería comprar el coche, **costara lo que costara**.

  He wanted to buy the car, no matter how much it cost.

- Repetition optional (= *whether...or not*, etc.)

  Puedes expresar tus opiniones, **seas o no (seas)** ciudadana.

  You can express your opinions whether you're a citizen or not.

  Teníamos que tomar esa clase nos **gustara o no (nos gustara)**.

  We had to take that clase, whether we liked it or not.

  Lo **hagas** ahora o (lo **hagas**) más tarde, tiene que estar hecho.

  Whether you do it now or later, it has to be done.